# GMAS
## GEORGIA MILESTONES ASSESSMENT SYSTEM

# GRADE 6
## ELA

Jason Reed

**First Edition**

# Table of Contents

# Introduction

**About the ELA GMAS Test**

The Grade 6 ELA test includes a variety of question types to assess different aspects of English Language Arts understanding. It consists of multiple-choice questions where students select the correct answer from the provided options, as well as open-ended questions that require students to explain their reasoning and problem-solving processes.

**About the ELA GMAS Practice Tests in This Book**

This book is designed to provide students with an accurate simulation of the GMAS tests. It includes practice tests that mirror the format, content, and time constraints of the actual GMAS test.

Repetition is a proven method for effective studying. We firmly believe in the power of practice, which is why we've included five carefully crafted practice tests in this book.

Practicing with these tests offers several benefits:

- **Improve Time Management:** Regular practice helps students become efficient in managing their time, ensuring they can complete all sections within the allocated time during the actual test.

- **Build Confidence:** Familiarity with the test format and question types boosts students' confidence, reducing anxiety on test day.

- **Identify Weaknesses:** These practice tests help pinpoint specific areas where students may need additional review and practice, allowing for targeted improvement.

- **Enhance Problem-Solving Skills:** Regular practice hones problem-solving skills and strategies, enabling students to tackle challenging questions more effectively.

- **Score Higher:** Focused practice and familiarity with the test structure equip students to aim for higher scores on the GMAS test.

The questions in these practice tests closely mirror those found in the actual GMAS tests, ensuring that your child gains a deep understanding of the test's structure and content. By working through these practice tests, they will be well-equipped to achieve success on the ELA GMAS test.

As parents, educators, or instructors, your support and encouragement play a pivotal role in your child's academic journey. We encourage you to actively engage with your child's ELA education, using these resources as tools to enhance their learning experience.

# Dear Parents,

Thank you for purchasing the GMAS Reading Practice Workbook for Grade 6.

As an independent author, I have put a great deal of effort into ensuring the quality and accuracy of the content provided. Each question has been carefully reviewed to provide the best learning experience.

However, despite the rigorous efforts to maintain high standards, occasional mistakes can occur. If you come across any errors or discrepancies in the book or the solutions, please do not hesitate to reach out. Your feedback is invaluable in helping to improve the quality of this workbook.

For any corrections, questions, or comments, please contact me at *jasonreedbooks@gmail.com*. Your assistance in identifying and rectifying any issues is greatly appreciated.

Thank you for your understanding and support.

Sincerely,

Jason Reed

# PRACTICE TEST 1

## GET STARTED →

**Read the article and answer the questions.**

### Chasing Dreams with Determination

Amara and her younger brother, Marcus, had grown up with the tales of the 1996 Atlanta Olympics. Their grandmother, Clara, would recount her experiences with such vivid detail that the kids felt like they had been there themselves. On many a warm evening, the family would gather in the cozy living room, where the flickering firelight seemed to make Clara's stories even more magical.

"It was like the world came to Georgia," Clara would say, her eyes twinkling with the memories. "The air was thick with hope and excitement. Every cheer from the crowd was like a heartbeat, pulsing through the city. I remember guiding athletes from distant lands, their faces a mix of nerves and dreams. And oh, the gymnastics! The way they soared and flipped—it was like watching poetry in motion."

One such evening, as Clara's words hung in the air, Amara felt a spark ignite within her. "One day," she whispered to herself, "I'll be part of something just as grand." That spark turned into determination when they heard that the 2024 Olympics would be held in Paris. The family gathered around, the room buzzing with excitement.

"Imagine seeing an Olympic athlete in person!" Marcus exclaimed, his eyes wide with wonder.

Their parents exchanged glances, the weight of practicality settling in. "It's a beautiful dream," their father said slowly. "But getting to Paris and securing tickets will be expensive. We'll need a solid plan."

Thus began their journey of preparation and perseverance. The family brainstormed ways to raise money, deciding on a series of community events. The bake sale was their first attempt. Amara and Marcus had spent hours in the kitchen, filling the house with the sweet aroma of cookies and cupcakes. But as they sat behind their table, watching people pass by without a second glance, their hope began to wane.

"This isn't working out as we planned," Amara sighed, her voice barely above a whisper. The unsold treats seemed to mock their efforts.

"We can't give up," Marcus replied, his young voice steady and sure. "We just need to find a way to get more people interested."

With renewed resolve, they upped their game. Colorful posters adorned local shop windows, and social media buzzed with their upcoming car wash event. This time, success followed. Cars lined up under the hot sun, and by the end of the day, their spirits and pockets were fuller.

Encouraged, they moved on to the talent show. The community rallied behind them, filling the evening with laughter, applause, and a shared sense of purpose. When the final count came in, they realized they had enough for their dream trip to Paris.

Arriving in Paris was like stepping into a dream. The city was a swirl of sights and sounds, its streets alive with the spirit of the Games. As they approached the arena, the enormity of their journey hit them. The place buzzed with an energy that felt almost tangible.

"Look at all of this!" Amara pointed, her heart pounding with excitement.

Her father smiled, a tear slipping down his cheek. "We did it, kids. We made it!"

Grandma Clara, standing beside them, her eyes misty with pride, squeezed their hands. "Your hard work and determination paid off," she said softly. "Just like in Atlanta, it's all about coming together and giving it your best."

As they watched their idols perform, the experience became more than just witnessing greatness. It was a testament to their journey, a proof of the power of dreams and determination. The 2024 Olympics in Paris became not just an event, but a cherished family memory, an echo of the hope and excitement that had once filled the air of Atlanta.

1. **Which one of the following sentences from the text does not contain a spelling mistake?**

   A) "The family brainstormed ways to raise money, deciding on a series of comunity events."

   B) "As they watched their idol perform, the experiance became more than just witnessing greatness."

   C) "Cars lined up under the hot sun, and by the end of the day, their sperits and pockets were fuller."

   D) "They made colorful posters, handed out flyers, and used social media to promote their next events."

2. **Which of the following best describes the setting where Clara shared her Olympic stories?**

   A) A park during a summer picnic

   B) The family's cozy living room with a flickering firelight

   C) A school auditorium during a presentation

   D) The local community center during an event

3. **What is the main reason the family initially struggles with their bake sale?**

   A) They did not make enough baked goods.

   B) They did not advertise the event well.

   C) They chose the wrong location for the sale.

   D) The weather was unfavorable.

4. **Based on the text, what can be inferred about the family's approach to achieving their goal of attending the 2024 Olympics in Paris?**

   A) They primarily relied on donations from neighbors to fund their trip.

   B) They adjusted their plans and tried different strategies after facing setbacks.

   C) They decided to use their savings when the bake sale didn't go as planned.

   D) They planned to sell personal items if their fundraising efforts were unsuccessful.

6

**5.** How does the community's response to the family's fundraising efforts change over time in the story?

- Ⓐ  The community remains uninterested in all the events.

- Ⓑ  The community only supports the bake sale event.

- Ⓒ  The community gradually becomes more supportive, particularly during the car wash and talent show.

- Ⓓ  The community supports the events equally from the beginning.

**6.** How does the family's approach to fundraising demonstrate their determination?

- Ⓐ  They sought financial help from relatives.

- Ⓑ  They gave up after the initial failure and tried different methods.

- Ⓒ  They remained persistent, trying new strategies to attract community support.

- Ⓓ  They used their own savings to make up for the shortfall in fundraising.

**7.** In the story, the phrase "the air was thick with hope and excitement" is used to describe the atmosphere during the 1996 Atlanta Olympics. What does the word "thick" most likely mean in this context?

- Ⓐ  Filled with a strong feeling

- Ⓑ  Filled with nostalgia

- Ⓒ  Hard to breathe

- Ⓓ  Crowded with people

**8.** Identify two main characters in the story and describe their roles in the family's effort to attend the 2024 Paris Olympics.

_____

_____

_____

_____

**9.** Analyze the impact of Clara's stories on Amara's motivation and actions throughout the story. Use specific details from the text to support your response.

_____

_____

_____

_____

_____

_____

_____

_____

_____

_____

_____

_____

_____

_____

_____

_____

_____

**10.** In the text, the author describes Grandma Clara's eyes as "twinkling with nostalgia" when she recalls her experiences at the 1996 Atlanta Olympics. What is the impact of this specific word choice on the meaning and tone of the passage? Use evidence from the text to support your response.

_____

_____

_____

_____

_____

_____

_____

_____

_____

_____

_____

_____

_____

_____

_____

_____

_____

_____

**Read the information and answer items 11 - 20.**

### The Fascinating World of Moon Jellyfish and Box Jellyfish

Jellyfish are fascinating sea creatures found in oceans all around the world. Two types of jellyfish that capture attention due to their unique characteristics are the Moon Jellyfish and the Box Jellyfish. The Moon Jellyfish, also known as Aurelia aurita, has a transparent, saucer-shaped bell that ranges from 10 to 16 inches in diameter, typically adorned with delicate patterns of lines and dots. Its short, fringe-like tentacles are situated around the edge of its bell, aiding in capturing small prey such as plankton.

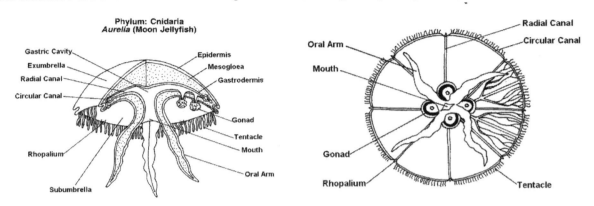

On the other hand, the Box Jellyfish, scientifically named Chironex fleckeri, is known for its box-shaped bell, which can also be around 10 inches in diameter but often grows larger. This jellyfish is notorious for its potent venom, with tentacles that extend from each of the four corners of its bell, reaching up to 10 feet in length.

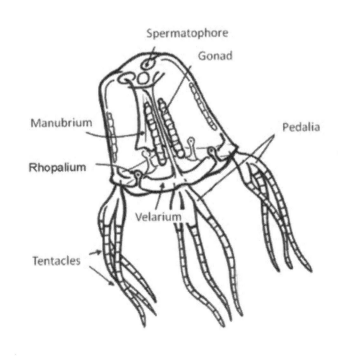

Both types of jellyfish have gelatinous bodies with tentacles, are found in oceans (especially warm waters), primarily feed on small marine organisms like plankton, and use a pulsating motion to propel themselves through the water. However, their distinctions are notable. The Moon Jellyfish's round, saucer-shaped bell contrasts with the Box Jellyfish's box-shaped bell. While the Moon Jellyfish generally has a smaller bell diameter, the Box Jellyfish's tentacles are significantly longer and more dangerous. The venom of the Moon Jellyfish is mild and usually harmless to humans, whereas the Box Jellyfish's venom can be extremely potent and even deadly.

Understanding these traits helps us appreciate the diversity and adaptability of these remarkable creatures. The Moon Jellyfish's gentle appearance and mild sting contrast sharply with the Box Jellyfish's potent venom and distinctive shape, showcasing the variety of survival strategies that jellyfish have developed in their ocean habitats.

11. **What is the shape of the Moon Jellyfish's bell?**

( A ) Box-shaped

( B ) Saucer-shaped

( C ) Cone-shaped

( D ) Oval-shaped

12. **What do Moon Jellyfish and Box Jellyfish primarily feed on?**

( A ) Fish

( B ) Crustaceans

( C ) Seaweed

( D ) Plankton

13. **Why might the Box Jellyfish be considered more dangerous to humans than the Moon Jellyfish?**

( A ) It is larger in size.

( B ) Its tentacles are longer.

( C ) Its venom is extremely potent and can be deadly.

( D ) It lives in deeper waters.

14. **How do the tentacles of the Moon Jellyfish and Box Jellyfish differ in their function?**

( A ) Both use tentacles for propulsion only.

( B ) Moon Jellyfish use short tentacles for capturing small prey, while Box Jellyfish have long tentacles that can deliver a potent sting.

( C ) Box Jellyfish often grow larger than the Moon Jellyfish.

( D ) Moon Jellyfish use tentacles to scare predators, while Box Jellyfish use them to blend into their environment.

**15.** In the context of the article, what does the word "gelatinous" most likely mean?

( A ) Having a jelly-like consistency

( B ) Having a hard texture

( C ) Smooth and shiny

( D ) Rough and spiky

**16.** Considering the differences in venom potency and tentacle length, how might the presence of Box Jellyfish and Moon Jellyfish in the same habitat impact the behavior and safety measures of swimmers and marine biologists working in those areas?

( A ) Both types of jellyfish would require similar safety measures due to their shared habitats.

( B ) Swimmers and marine biologists might prioritize avoiding areas known for Box Jellyfish due to their more dangerous venom while being less cautious in areas with Moon Jellyfish.

( C ) The presence of Moon Jellyfish would necessitate more stringent safety measures due to their longer tentacles.

( D ) The venom of both jellyfish types is equally dangerous, so safety measures would be the same regardless of which jellyfish is present.

**17.** Read the passage below and identify the word that is spelled incorrectly.

The Moon Jellyfish, also known as Aurelia aurita, has a transparent, saucer-shaped bell. It captures small prey like plankton with its fring-like tentacles. The Box Jellyfish, or Chironex fleckeri, has a box-shaped bell and potent venom. Its long tentacles can reach up to 10 feet.

( A ) transparent

( B ) captures

( C ) fringe

( D ) potent

**18.** Explain how the tentacles of the Moon Jellyfish and the Box Jellyfish differ in both appearance and function. Use details from the text to support your answer.

_____

_____

_____

_____

_____

_____

_____

_____

_____

_____

**19.** Considering the unique characteristics of the Moon Jellyfish and the Box Jellyfish, discuss how these features might influence their survival strategies in their natural habitats. Provide examples from the text to support your explanation.

_____

_____

_____

_____

_____

_____

_____

_____

_____

_____

_____

**20.** Given the differences in the shape, size, and venom potency of Moon Jellyfish and Box Jellyfish, how might these differences affect their roles in their respective ecosystems and their interactions with other marine life? Discuss how these characteristics might influence their predatory behaviors, the potential threats they pose to other species, and their overall ecological impact. Provide examples to support your answer.

_____

_____

_____

_____

_____

_____

_____

_____

_____

_____

_____

_____

_____

_____

_____

_____

_____

**Whispers in the Garden**

In the garden, green and bright,
Plants reach up to touch the light.
From the ground, they grow so tall,
Spring and summer, through it all.

Roots dig deep, so strong and wide,
In the earth, they quietly hide.
They drink water, sip by sip
, From the soil, a gentle drip.

Leaves that shimmer in the sun,
Catch the light, the work begun.
Turning sunlight into food,
With a magic science mood.

Flowers bloom in colors bold,
Red and purple, blue and gold.
Bees and butterflies take flight,
Spreading pollen day and night.

Some plants give us food to eat,
Fruits and veggies, oh so sweet.
Tomatoes red and carrots long,
In our gardens, they belong.

Others shade us from the heat,
Trees with branches, oh so neat.
They clean the air, they give us wood,
Standing tall as they should.

Every plant, both small and grand,
Has a job, a place to stand.
They whisper secrets in the breeze,
Of nature's wonders, such as these.

So when you walk among the green,
Remember all the things you've seen.
Plants are life, and life they give,
In the garden, where we live.

16

# The Secret of Green Valley

In Green Valley, the sun rose, casting a golden glow over lush gardens and tall trees. Every morning, young Emma would race outside to tend to her garden. Today, she noticed something unusual.

"Mom! Dad! Come quickly!" Emma shouted, her eyes wide with excitement. Her parents hurried over.

"What is it, Emma?" her dad asked.

"Look at these flowers!" Emma pointed to vibrant blooms that hadn't been there the day before. The petals glistened with dew, reflecting the soft morning light like tiny jewels.

"I think they're special," Emma said, pride swelling in her chest. "Maybe they grew because I've been taking such good care of the garden."

Just then, they heard a rustling in the bushes. Out stepped Mr. Green, the elderly gardener. "Morning, Johnson family," he greeted. "I see you've discovered some new blooms."

"Mr. Green, these flowers are beautiful," Emma said. "But I'm worried about the trees in the old forest. They look sad and weak. What can we do to help them?"

Mr. Green looked serious. "The forest has been struggling. Too many weeds and fallen branches are blocking sunlight and nutrients."

"We need to help them, Dad. Can we?" Emma asked.

"Of course we can," Mr. Johnson said.

The family, along with Mr. Green, walked to the forest. The air was thick with the scent of damp earth and decaying leaves. Thick weeds and fallen branches covered the forest floor, suffocating the life out of the undergrowth.

"We need to clear these out," Mr. Green said. "It'll take some hard work, but we can do it together."

Emma and her parents got to work, pulling weeds and moving branches. Emma's hands grew dirty, her arms tired, but she kept going, driven by a sense of purpose. The forest seemed to breathe easier with each weed pulled, each branch moved.

By the afternoon, the forest floor was transformed. Sunlight streamed through the canopy, illuminating the now-clear ground. The trees stood taller, their leaves rustling in relief.

"We did it," Emma said, smiling.

Mr. Green nodded. "The trees will be much happier now. You've given them a chance to thrive."

Emma felt a deep connection with the world around her. She knew that by caring for the garden and the forest, she was part of something bigger, something beautiful and essential.

From that day on, Green Valley flourished more than ever. The plants and trees thrived, and Emma felt a deep connection with every leaf and petal, knowing she was making a difference.

**21.** What do the plants in the garden reach up to touch?

- (A) The sky
- (B) The light
- (C) The wind
- (D) The rain

**22.** Which creatures are mentioned as spreading pollen in the garden?

- (A) Birds and bees
- (B) Ants and butterflies
- (C) Bees and butterflies
- (D) Flies and beetles

**23.** Why might the poem say that plants "whisper secrets in the breeze"?

- (A) Because plants can talk to each other.
- (B) The wind whistles as it blows through the leaves.
- (C) Because the plants move their leaves quickly.
- (D) Because the sound of leaves rustling in the wind is gentle and quiet.

**24.** Why does the poem emphasize that every plant, both small and grand, has a job?

- (A) To highlight the diverse contributions of all plants to the environment.
- (B) To indicate that plants compete with each other for resources.
- (C) To suggest that small plants are more important than large plants.
- (D) To show that only large plants are important.

18

**25.** How does the poem "Whispers in the Garden" and the story "The Secret of Green Valley" both emphasize the importance of caring for plants and nature?

(A) Both highlight the scientific processes plants use to grow.

(B) Both illustrate the beauty and colors of flowers.

(C) Both show characters actively involved in taking care of plants and the environment.

(D) Both discuss the different types of plants that provide food.

**26.** Considering both the poem "Whispers in the Garden" and the story "The Secret of Green Valley," why might the author have chosen to include both the garden and the forest settings?

(A) Both show how plants grow in different places.

(B) To illustrate that both cultivated and wild areas of nature require human effort to maintain their health and beauty.

(C) To highlight that forests and gardens grow different types of plants that provide for humans.

(D) To demonstrate that gardens are easier to take care of than forests.

**27.** What lesson about responsibility and community can be drawn from Emma's family's efforts in "The Secret of Green Valley" in comparison to the general care described in "Whispers in the Garden"?

(A) Responsibility for nature is a task that should only be handled by professionals.

(B) Community efforts are only needed when there is a visible problem.

(C) Individual efforts in the garden are as important as community efforts in the forest.

(D) Caring for the environment is a communal effort that requires the involvement of everyone, regardless of their age or expertise.

**28.** How does the poem "Whispers in the Garden" enhance the reader's understanding of the environmental challenges faced by the characters in "The Secret of Green Valley"?

(A) The poem's focus on the delicate balance of nature and the importance of each plant's role helps readers understand why Emma's family must work to clear the forest floor and support the trees.

(B) The poem provides a detailed description of the types of plants in the garden, helping readers identify the plants in the story.

(C) The poem describes the specific ways of gardening, which are also mentioned in the story.

(D) The poem discusses the different seasons in which plants grow, which helps explain the timing of events in the story.

**29.** Read the following excerpts from the poem and the story. Based on these excerpts, select the best description of Emma's character traits.

Excerpt from the Poem: "Roots dig deep, so strong and wide, In the earth, they quietly hide. They drink water, sip by sip, From the soil, a gentle drip."

Excerpt from the Story: "Emma's hands grew dirty, her arms tired, but she kept going, driven by a sense of purpose. She could feel the forest breathing easier with each weed pulled, each branch moved."

Which of the following best describes Emma's character traits?

A  Lazy and uninterested

B  Determined and caring

C  Indifferent and distracted

D  Anxious and fearful

**30.** Provide details from the poem that support your chosen description of Emma's character traits.

_____

_____

_____

_____

_____

_____

_____

_____

_____

_____

_____

_____

_____

## Text 1: Newspaper Article - The Bright Future of Space Exploration
By Sally Dover, Science Correspondent

In recent years, space exploration has become a beacon of hope and progress for humanity. As we look towards the stars, the benefits of exploring the cosmos become increasingly clear.

One of the most significant advantages of space exploration is the expansion of our scientific knowledge. Missions to distant planets and celestial bodies provide invaluable data that help us understand the origins of our solar system and the potential for life beyond Earth. For instance, the Mars rovers have uncovered essential information about the Red Planet's geology and climate, offering clues about its history and potential for sustaining life.

Moreover, space exploration drives technological innovation. The technologies developed for space missions, such as satellite communications, GPS, and advanced medical devices, have found applications in everyday life, significantly improving our quality of living. These innovations demonstrate how the pursuit of space exploration benefits society as a whole.

Additionally, the inspirational value of space exploration cannot be overstated. It sparks curiosity and encourages students to pursue careers in science, technology, engineering, and mathematics (STEM). The achievements of astronauts and space missions serve as powerful motivators for young minds, fostering a culture of innovation and excellence.

As we continue to explore the cosmos, the potential for further discoveries and advancements grows. Space exploration is not just about satisfying our curiosity; it's about pushing the boundaries of human knowledge and capability. The benefits extend far beyond the confines of our planet, contributing significantly to the betterment of humanity.

In conclusion, space exploration is essential for scientific progress, technological advancement, and educational inspiration. As we invest in the future of space travel, we invest in the future of humanity itself.

## Text 2: Newspaper Article - The Hidden Costs of Space Exploration
By Ben Wilson, Environmental Analyst

While the allure of space exploration captivates many, it is crucial to examine the significant drawbacks that come with venturing into the cosmos. The high costs, environmental impact, and risks to human life are serious concerns that warrant careful consideration.

One of the most pressing issues is the **astronomical** cost of space missions. Billions of dollars are funneled into space programs, diverting funds from critical issues on Earth such as poverty, healthcare, and education. Critics argue that these areas should be prioritized over the exploration of other planets, where immediate benefits to humanity are uncertain.

Environmental concerns also loom large over space exploration. Rocket launches contribute to atmospheric pollution, adding to the already critical levels of greenhouse gases. Additionally, space debris from **defunct** satellites and abandoned spacecraft poses a growing threat to both future missions and our planet. The environmental footprint of space travel is a significant drawback that cannot be ignored.

Moreover, the risks to human life involved in space exploration are substantial. Astronauts face numerous dangers, including exposure to harmful radiation, the potential for equipment failure, and the psychological challenges of long-duration missions. The ethical implications of risking human lives for the sake of exploration raise serious questions about the justification of such missions.

In conclusion, the drawbacks of space exploration, including its high costs, environmental impact, and risks to human life, outweigh its benefits. While the pursuit of knowledge and technological advancement is important, it is essential to address and prioritize the pressing issues we face on Earth. Only then can we responsibly consider the expansion of our reach into the cosmos?

The debate over space exploration continues, but it is clear that a balanced approach is necessary to ensure that we do not overlook the needs of our planet and its inhabitants in our quest to explore the stars.

**31.** What does the word "beacon" mean in the context of the article "The Bright Future of Space Exploration"?

(A) A type of satellite

(B) A warning signal

(C) A source of inspiration

(D) A silver lining

**32.** In the article "The Hidden Costs of Space Exploration," what does "astronomical" most closely mean?

(A) Related to stars

(B) Very large or expensive

(C) Concerning rockets

(D) Relating to Astronomy

**33.** What does "defunct" mean in the context of the article "The Hidden Costs of Space Exploration"?

(A) Broken and not working

(B) Very advanced

(C) Dangerous

(D) Newly built

**34.** What is one of the significant advantages of space exploration mentioned in the article?

A. Reduces Earthly pollution

B. Expands scientific knowledge

C. Decreases poverty

D. Eliminates space debris

**35.** According to the text, what is one reason critics argue against space exploration?

A. It guarantees economic benefits.

B. It provides no technological advancements.

C. It involves high costs and diverts funds from critical Earthly issues.

D. It has no environmental impact.

**36.** Based on the article, why might some people support space exploration despite its high costs?

A. They believe it reduces environmental pollution.

B. They think it has no risks involved.

C. They argue that technological innovations from space missions benefit daily life.

D. They feel it addresses immediate social issues.

**37.** Evaluate the arguments presented in both texts about space exploration. Which of the following best represents a balanced approach that considers both the benefits and drawbacks?

A. Allocate all resources to space exploration, ignoring pressing Earthly problems.

B. Halt all space exploration activities to focus entirely on Earthly issues.

C. Only conduct space missions that have no associated risks to human life.

D. Continue investing in space exploration while also increasing efforts to address environmental and social issues on Earth.

**38.** Based on the articles, discuss one significant benefit and one major drawback of space exploration. How do these points contribute to the overall debate about whether humanity should prioritize space exploration or focus on addressing Earthly issues?

_____

_____

_____

_____

_____

_____

_____

_____

_____

_____

_____

_____

**39.** Based on the articles, how does space exploration serve as an inspiration for students to pursue STEM careers? Why might this be considered an important benefit, despite the high costs and risks associated with space exploration?

_____

_____

_____

_____

_____

_____

_____

_____

_____

_____

**40.** In recent discussions about the future of space exploration, two contrasting perspectives have emerged. One view highlights the significant benefits of space exploration, such as advancing scientific knowledge, driving technological innovation, and inspiring educational pursuits. Conversely, the other perspective focuses on the drawbacks, including the high costs, environmental impact, and risks to human life associated with space missions.

**Essay Prompt:** Should humanity prioritize space exploration despite its high costs, environmental impact, and risks to human life, or should we focus on addressing pressing issues on Earth first? Develop an argumentative essay supporting your position with reasons and evidence from the texts provided.

**Guidelines for Your Essay:**

- Clearly state your position on whether space exploration should be prioritized.
- Use specific reasons and evidence from the texts to support your argument.
- Address and refute the opposing viewpoint to strengthen your argument.
- Organize your essay with an introduction, body paragraphs, and a conclusion.
- Use proper grammar, punctuation, and spelling throughout your essay.

_____

_____

_____

_____

_____

_____

_____

_____

**Read the information text and answer questions 41 - 51**

### The Influence of Social Media

In today's digital age, social media has become integral to daily life, influencing how people communicate, share information, and perceive the world. This powerful tool offers numerous benefits and presents challenges that are essential to understand, especially for students navigating the online world.

One of social media's most significant positive influences is its ability to connect people. Platforms like Facebook, Instagram, and Twitter provide instant communication tools, enabling individuals to stay in touch with family and friends regardless of geographical distance. This ease of communication fosters stronger relationships and helps maintain social bonds. Additionally, social media serves as a powerful tool for disseminating information. News, educational content, and current events are readily available, often in real-time. Platforms such as YouTube and educational pages on Facebook and Instagram offer valuable resources for learning and staying informed. Social media also allows individuals to express themselves creatively. Whether through writing, photography, or video, platforms like TikTok and Instagram give users a space to showcase their talents and share their passions with a broader audience, boosting self-esteem and encouraging creative growth.

However, social media also has its drawbacks. It can be a breeding ground for negative behavior, such as cyberbullying and online harassment. Cyberbullying involves using digital platforms to harass or intimidate others, leading to severe emotional distress and impacting mental health, particularly among young users. Furthermore, the rapid spread of information on social media can sometimes lead to the dissemination of false or misleading information. Misinformation, or fake news, can cause confusion and spread panic, making it essential for users to critically evaluate the sources of information they encounter online. Another significant issue is the potential for addiction and distraction. Social media can be highly addictive, leading to excessive screen time and distraction from important activities such as studying, physical exercise, and face-to-face interactions, which can impact academic performance and overall well-being.

The influence of social media on society is profound and multifaceted. While it offers numerous benefits, it also presents challenges. By understanding these influences, people can make informed decisions about their social media use, balancing the positives while mitigating the negatives. It is crucial to approach social media with awareness and responsibility to harness its benefits while minimizing its drawbacks.

**41.** **What are the two benefits of social media mentioned in the text?**

(A) Making videos and posting pictures

(B) Instant communication and creative expression

(C) Misinformation and distraction

(D) To quickly spread information

**42.** Why is it important to critically evaluate the sources of information encountered online according to the text?

( A ) To make sure it is entertaining

( B ) To avoid spending too much time on social media

( C ) To prevent the spread of misinformation and panic

( D ) To prevent cyberbullying

**43.** Which of the following best describes the term "cyberbullying" as used in the passage?

( A ) Using digital platforms to harass others.

( B ) Using social media to spread false information.

( C ) Using online tools to physically hurt others.

( D ) Using the internet to share personal content of others.

**44.** What impact can cyberbullying have on young users, based on the information in the text?

( A ) It can increase their screen time

( B ) It can lead to severe emotional distress and impact mental health

( C ) It can distract from their academic performance

( D ) It can lead to social isolation

**45.** According to the text, how can social media affect academic performance and overall well-being?

( A ) Distraction from important activities

( B ) By providing fake news

( C ) By discouraging students from studying

( D ) Allowing instant communication with family and friends

**46.** Analyze how social media's ability to connect people can also lead to challenges. Which of the following best explains this dual effect?

A  It allows people to share creative content but can also lead to plagiarism.

B  It helps maintain social bonds but can also spread misinformation.

C  It provides real-time news but can cause addiction.

D  It enables instant communication but can also facilitate cyberbullying.

**47.** Evaluate the statement: "Social media serves as a powerful tool for disseminating information." What evidence from the text supports this claim?

A  Instant communication for better collaboration

B  Platforms like YouTube and educational pages on Facebook offer valuable resources for learning.

C  Instagram and TikTok promote educational resources

D  Misinformation can spread quickly on social media.

**48.** Construct an argument based on the text about the importance of balancing social media use, including both its benefits and challenges. Which statement best supports this balanced view?

A  Social media is entirely beneficial and should be used as much as possible.

B  The drawbacks of social media outweigh the benefits, so it should be avoided.

C  By understanding the influences of social media, people can make informed decisions to harness its benefits while minimizing its drawbacks.

D  Social media's ability to connect people makes it more important than any potential negatives.

**49.** Based on the text, design a plan for a school project where students will research the effects of social media on their peers. What would be the most effective first step in ensuring a comprehensive and balanced study?

A  Collect stories from peers about their personal experiences with social media.

B  Organize a debate on whether social media is beneficial or harmful.

C  Have students write essays about their own use of social media.

D  Create a survey that includes questions about both the positive and negative impacts of social media.

29

**50.** Explain two positive influences of social media mentioned in the passage and how they benefit individuals.

_____

_____

_____

_____

_____

_____

_____

_____

_____

_____

**51.** Describe two challenges of social media discussed in the passage and explain why they are important for users to understand.

_____

_____

_____

_____

_____

_____

_____

_____

# Answers Test Practice 1

1. D. "They made colorful posters, handed out flyers, and used social media to promote their next events."
2. B. The family's cozy living room with a flickering firelight
3. B. They did not advertise the event well
4. B. They adjusted their plans and tried different strategies after facing setbacks.
5. C. The community gradually becomes more supportive, particularly during the car wash and talent show.
6. C. They remained persistent, trying new strategies to attract community support.
7. A. Filled with a strong feeling
8. **Amara:** Amara is one of the main characters who is determined to attend the 2024 Paris Olympics. She actively participates in organizing and executing the fundraising events with her family.
**Grandma Clara:** Grandma Clara is another key character who inspires the family with her stories about volunteering at the 1996 Atlanta Olympics. Her memories and encouragement motivate the family to pursue their dream.
9. Clara's stories about the 1996 Atlanta Olympics serve as the initial inspiration for Amara's dream. Clara's vivid recounting of the event fills Amara with a sense of possibility and excitement, which is evident when Amara whispers to herself that she wants to be part of something grand. This inspiration is what drives Amara to embark on the journey to attend the 2024 Paris Olympics. Despite initial setbacks, like the unsuccessful bake sale, Amara's motivation does not wane. Encouraged by Marcus, she refocuses her efforts, leading to successful fundraising events like the car wash and talent show. Clara's stories ultimately instill in Amara a sense of determination and the belief that dreams can be achieved through hard work and perseverance.
10. The phrase "twinkling with nostalgia" suggests a sense of warmth and fond remembrance, which creates a sentimental and affectionate tone in the passage. This word choice highlights Grandma Clara's deep emotional connection to her memories of the Olympics, emphasizing how meaningful and treasured these experiences are to her. The use of "twinkling" evokes an image of her eyes shining with joy and affection, which adds a layer of emotional depth to the narrative.
11. B. Saucer-shaped
12. D. Plankton
13. C. Its venom is extremely potent and can be deadly.
14. B. Moon Jellyfish use short tentacles for capturing small prey, while Box Jellyfish have long tentacles that can deliver a potent sting.
15. A. Having a jelly-like consistency
16. B. Swimmers and marine biologists might prioritize avoiding areas known for Box Jellyfish due to their more dangerous venom while being less cautious in areas with Moon Jellyfish.
17. C. Fringe
18. The Moon Jellyfish has short, fringe-like tentacles that are situated around the edge of its saucer-shaped bell. These tentacles are used to capture small prey such as plankton. In contrast, the Box Jellyfish has long tentacles that can reach up to 10 feet, extending from each of the four corners of its box-shaped bell. These tentacles are highly venomous and can capture larger prey, like small fish and crustaceans, making the Box Jellyfish a more formidable predator.
19. The Moon Jellyfish's short, fringe-like tentacles and mild venom allow it to capture small prey like plankton, making it an effective predator of tiny marine organisms. Its transparent, saucer-shaped bell helps it blend into its environment, providing some protection from predators. On the other hand, the Box Jellyfish's long, potent tentacles and box-shaped bell make it a more formidable predator, capable of capturing larger prey. Its potent venom also deters potential predators, enhancing its survival. These features allow the Box Jellyfish to dominate its habitat, as its venomous tentacles pose a significant threat to both prey and predators, influencing the behavior and distribution of other marine species in its vicinity.
20. The Moon Jellyfish and Box Jellyfish play different roles in their ecosystems due to their physical characteristics and venom potency. The Moon Jellyfish, with its mild venom and saucer-shaped bell, primarily preys on plankton and serves as prey for larger marine animals like sea turtles. It helps control plankton populations, supporting the marine food web.
In contrast, the Box Jellyfish, with its potent venom and box-shaped bell, is a formidable predator, capturing larger prey such as small fish and crustaceans. Its presence can cause other marine species to avoid areas where it lives, altering local marine life behavior. The dangerous venom also requires humans to take strict safety precautions, affecting activities like swimming and research in areas inhabited by Box Jellyfish. This potent venom and long tentacles make it a significant threat to both marine life and humans, impacting the ecosystem more drastically than the Moon Jellyfish.

21. B. The light
22. C. Bees and butterflies
23. D. Because the sound of leaves rustling in the wind is gentle and quiet.
24. A. To highlight the diverse contributions of all plants to the environment.
25. C. Both show characters actively involved in taking care of plants and the environment.
26. B. To illustrate that both cultivated and wild areas of nature require human effort to maintain their health and beauty.
27. D. Caring for the environment is a communal effort that requires the involvement of everyone, regardless of their age or expertise.
28. A. The poem's focus on the delicate balance of nature and the importance of each plant's role helps readers understand why Emma's family must work to clear the forest floor and support the trees.
29. B. Determined and caring
30. In the poem, the lines "Roots dig deep, so strong and wide, In the earth, they quietly hide" reflect Emma's determination and strong foundation in her commitment to caring for her garden. The metaphor of roots digging deep and drinking water "sip by sip" symbolizes her patience and careful attention to detail. Emma's continuous effort to nurture her plants demonstrates her caring nature. This is further supported by her dedication in the story, where despite getting tired, she continues to work hard to help the forest thrive. Both texts highlight her perseverance and compassionate attitude towards nature.
31. C. A source of inspiration
32. B. Very large or expensive
33. A. Broken and not working
34. B. Expands scientific knowledge
35. C. it involves high costs and diverts funds from critically Earthly issues
36. C. They argue that technological innovations from space missions benefit daily life.
37. D. continue investing in space exploration while also increasing efforts to address environmental and social issies on Earth.
38. **Identifies one significant benefit of space exploration (1 point):**
● Example: Expands scientific knowledge, drives technological innovation, or inspires educational pursuits.
**Identifies one major drawback of space exploration (1 point):**
● Example: High costs, environmental impact, or risks to human life.
**Explains how the identified benefit contributes to the argument for prioritizing space exploration (1 point):**
● Example: The benefit demonstrates the potential long-term advantages and advancements that can improve life on Earth.

**Explains how the identified drawback contributes to the argument against prioritizing space exploration (1 point):**
- Example: The drawback highlights immediate concerns and issues that need addressing to ensure responsible and ethical use of resources.

**Provides a clear and logical connection between the benefit and drawback in the context of the overall debate (1 point):**
- Example: Balancing the potential benefits with the immediate drawbacks helps in understanding the complexity of the decision.

39. **Describes how space exploration inspires students to pursue STEM careers (1 point):**
- Example: Highlights the role of astronauts and space missions in sparking curiosity and interest in science and technology.

**Explains why this inspirational value is considered an important benefit (1 point):**
- Example: Discusses the long-term impact on education, innovation, and future technological advancements.

**Connects the inspirational value to the broader debate about space exploration (1 point):**
- Example: Balances the high costs and risks by emphasizing the potential for developing a skilled workforce and fostering a culture of innovation.

40. Introduction (1 point)
- Clearly introduces the topic and provides context.
- States the writer's position on whether humanity should prioritize space exploration or focus on Earthly issues.

Thesis Statement (1 point)
- Presents a clear and concise thesis statement that articulates the writer's stance.

Supporting Arguments (2 points)
- Provides at least two strong, well-developed supporting arguments for the writer's position.
- Uses specific evidence and examples from the provided texts to support each argument.
- Clearly explains how the evidence supports the argument. 4. Counterarguments and Rebuttals (1 point)
- Identifies and addresses at least one counterargument or opposing viewpoint.
- Provides a thoughtful and logical rebuttal to the counterargument using evidence from the texts.

Use of Textual Evidence (1 point)
- Integrates relevant quotes and evidence from the provided texts to support arguments and rebuttals.
- Properly cites sources to strengthen the writer's position. 6. Organization and Coherence (1 point)
- Essay is well-organized with a clear introduction, body paragraphs, and conclusion.
- Each paragraph flows logically and transitions smoothly to the next.
- Ideas are presented in a coherent and logical sequence.

Conclusion (1 point)
- Summarizes the main points and reinforces the thesis statement.
- Provides a strong closing statement that leaves a lasting impression on the reader.
- May suggest broader implications or future considerations regarding the topic.

Total Points: 7

41. B. Instant communication and creative expression
42. C. To prevent the spread of misinformation and panic
43. A. Using digital platforms to harass others.
44. B. It can lead to severe emotional distress and impact mental health
45. A. Distraction from important activities
46. D. It enables instant communication but can also facilitate cyberbullying.
47. B. Platforms like YouTube and educational pages on Facebook offer valuable resources for learning.
48. C. By understanding the influences of social media, people can make informed decisions to harness its benefits while minimizing its drawbacks.
49. D. Create a survey that includes questions about both the positive and negative impacts of social media.
50. **Connecting People**: Social media platforms like Facebook, Instagram, and Twitter allow individuals to stay in touch with family and friends regardless of geographical distance. This ease of communication fosters stronger relationships and helps maintain social bonds.
**Disseminating Information**: Social media serves as a powerful tool for sharing news, educational content, and current events in real-time. Platforms such as YouTube and educational pages on Facebook and Instagram offer valuable resources for learning and staying informed.
51. **Cyberbullying**: The passage highlights that social media can be a breeding ground for negative behavior, such as cyberbullying, where individuals use digital platforms to harass or intimidate others. This can lead to severe emotional distress and impact mental health, particularly among young users.
**Spread of Misinformation**: The rapid spread of information on social media can sometimes lead to the dissemination of false or misleading information. Misinformation, or fake news, can cause confusion and spread panic. It is important for users to critically evaluate the sources of information they encounter online to avoid these negative effects.

# PRACTICE TEST 2

GET STARTED →

## The Hidden Journal

In the summer of 1865, Georgia was a place of quiet recovery. Twelve-year-old Clara Thompson, with her fiery red hair and bright green eyes, stood on the porch of her family's small wooden house, watching the sunset behind the rolling hills.

One hot afternoon, Clara wandered deep into the woods behind her home. Her explorations led her to a hidden path, overgrown with vines and wildflowers, which eventually opened up to an old, abandoned cabin. Curiosity propelled her inside, where she found a dusty leather-bound journal on a rickety table.

The journal belonged to Abigail Turner, who had lived through the tumultuous years of the Civil War. Abigail's entries, written in elegant script, recounted secret meetings and coded messages. She had been a spy, gathering information and risking her life to aid the Union Army. The journal mentioned important figures like General Sherman and President Lincoln, though never directly. Clara pieced together the significance from the subtle hints in Abigail's words.

With a newfound sense of purpose, Clara decided to use the lessons from Abigail's journal to help her struggling town. She organized efforts to rebuild dilapidated buildings, plant new crops, and set up makeshift schools. People from neighboring towns, drawn by the quiet determination in Clara's actions, began to join her.

Clara's father, Samuel, who had returned from the war with a limp from the Battle of Atlanta, watched his daughter with pride. He quietly supported her efforts, offering advice and labor when needed, despite his injury.

One evening, the townspeople gathered around a bonfire. Clara shared passages from Abigail's journal, letting the words paint a picture of the past. She read about the hardships, the small acts of courage, and the unspoken bonds that had held people together during the war. As she read, the crowd fell silent, each person lost in their thoughts.

Years passed, and the town transformed. The fields were lush with crops, new homes stood tall, and children attended school. Clara grew into a young woman whose quiet strength inspired everyone around her. One day, while working in her garden, Clara discovered a small metal box buried beneath the soil. Inside was a medal of honor, awarded to Abigail Turner for her bravery.

Clara held the medal, feeling a deep connection to Abigail, the woman whose hidden words had changed her life. She realized that the courage and resilience shown in the past had woven itself into the fabric of their community.

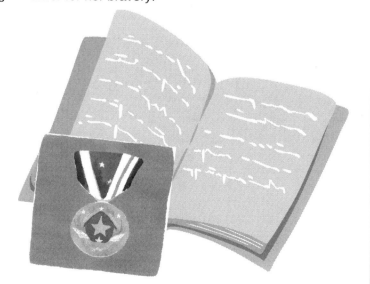

The townspeople never spoke directly of the hardships they had endured or the quiet heroism they witnessed. Instead, they found strength in their shared history and unspoken understanding. The story of Clara Thompson and the hidden journal became a subtle reminder of the power of bravery, unity, and the enduring spirit of Georgia.

1. **What does the word "abandoned" in the context of the story most likely mean?**

   - (A) Stranded and isolated
   - (B) Uninhabited and left behind
   - (C) Recently visited
   - (D) Hidden and forsaken

2. **In the story, what does the word "determination" best describe about Clara's character?**

   - (A) Her physical strength and stamina
   - (B) Her curiosity about the woods
   - (C) Her strong resolve to help her community
   - (D) Her single-minded approach

3. **Which of the following is the correct spelling of the word that means "a deep feeling of sadness"?**

   - (A) Grief
   - (B) Greef
   - (C) Greif
   - (D) Grif

4. **Who was mentioned in Abigail Turner's journal as a significant figure during the Civil War?**

   - (A) General Sherman
   - (B) President George Washington
   - (C) Clara's father
   - (D) Abraham Lincoln

**5.** Why did Clara decide to help her community after reading Abigail's journal?

( A ) She wanted to gain attention.

( B ) She wanted to make a difference.

( C ) She felt a sense of duty to Abigail.

( D ) She was inspired by Abigail's bravery.

**6.** How did the townspeople react to Clara reading passages from Abigail's journal around the bonfire?

( A ) They continued their conversations.

( B ) They were silent.

( C ) They politely listened.

( D ) They connected their past struggles to their own experiences.

**7.** What can be inferred about the impact of Abigail's journal on Clara's community from their reaction to the bonfire and subsequent actions?

( A ) The community felt obligated to listen to Clara because of her father's influence.

( B ) The stories in Abigail's journal motivated the community to rebuild and strengthen their town.

( C ) The community was inspired by Clara's leadership and decided to support her efforts.

( D ) The journal reminded the community of their hardships, leading them to appreciate their current lives more.

**8.** How did Clara's discovery of Abigail's journal influence her actions and decisions throughout the story?

( A ) Clara was inspired by Abigail's courage, leading her to take the initiative in rebuilding her community.

( B ) Clara decided to share Abigail's stories with the townspeople to keep history alive.

( C ) Clara became motivated to improve her skills and knowledge about the war.

( D ) Clara used the journal to understand more about the history of her town.

36

9. **How might the themes of bravery and community in Clara's story inspire students today to address challenges in their own communities, and what actions could they take?**

A  Students might recognize the importance of historical knowledge.

B  Students could be inspired to form groups to identify and tackle local issues, demonstrating leadership and teamwork.

C  Students might focus on their personal goals.

D  Students could write their own stories about local heroes to share with their community, fostering a sense of pride and connection.

10. **How does the use of the word "resilience" describe the townspeople's ability to recover from hardships?**

A  The word "resilience" suggests the townspeople easily give up when faced with challenges.

B  The word "resilience" indicates the townspeople were passionate about changing their situation.

C  The word "resilience" highlights the townspeople's strength and ability to overcome difficulties.

D  The word "resilience" means the townspeople were able to easily overcome the effects of the war without any hard work.

**Read the information text and answer items 11 - 20.**

---

**Weather Patterns Around the World**

Weather is the condition of the atmosphere at any given time, encompassing phenomena such as sunshine, precipitation, wind, and temperature. Various regions of the world experience distinct weather patterns, influenced by their geographic location and atmospheric conditions.

Sunny weather occurs when solar radiation is abundant, with minimal cloud cover, typically resulting in warm or hot temperatures. This is common in regions like Georgia during the summer months. Precipitation in the form of rain occurs when atmospheric water vapor condenses into droplets that fall to the ground. Rain can range from drizzles to heavy downpours, essential for plant growth and replenishing water bodies.

Snowy weather is characterized by temperatures below freezing, causing atmospheric moisture to crystallize into snowflakes, which accumulate on the ground. This phenomenon is typical in colder regions such as Alaska or mountainous areas. Windy conditions arise from the movement of air masses due to differences in atmospheric pressure, which can make temperatures feel cooler and are often observed in coastal or open-plan areas.

Various regions experience distinct weather patterns. Tropical regions, located near the equator, such as Brazil and Indonesia, maintain consistently warm temperatures year-round and typically have two primary seasons: a wet season with significant rainfall and a dry season with minimal precipitation. Desert regions, like Arizona in the USA and the Sahara Desert in Africa, receive very little rainfall, with extreme temperature variations between hot days and cool nights. Polar regions, including Antarctica and the Arctic, are characterized by frigid temperatures, ice, and snow, with prolonged winters and brief summers. Temperate regions, such as Georgia in the USA, experience four distinct seasons—spring, summer, autumn (fall), and winter—resulting in a wide range of weather conditions throughout the year.

---

Recent extreme weather events have been linked to climate change, which is driven by increased concentrations of greenhouse gases in the atmosphere due to human activities like fossil fuel combustion and deforestation. For instance, Europe experienced an unprecedented heatwave in 2023, with temperatures exceeding 40°C in Italy, leading to health crises and wildfires. Climate models suggest that global warming is increasing the frequency and intensity of heat waves.

In South Asia, countries like India and Bangladesh faced severe flooding in 2022 due to exceptionally heavy monsoon rains. These extreme precipitation events are attributed to climate change, which is intensifying the hydrological cycle and increasing the likelihood of such occurrences.

In the United States, the frequency and intensity of hurricanes have risen, exemplified by Hurricane Ida in 2021. This hurricane caused extensive damage in Louisiana and brought heavy rainfall and flooding to the northeastern states. Warmer sea surface temperatures, a consequence of climate change, are enhancing the power of tropical cyclones.

Understanding weather patterns and their changes is vital for preparing for diverse weather conditions and comprehending the implications of climate change. This knowledge enables communities and policymakers to develop strategies to mitigate the impacts of extreme weather events and protect populations and ecosystems. Awareness of weather patterns is crucial for our daily lives and aids in understanding the broader environmental changes occurring around us.

**11.** **What does "precipitation" refer to in weather terms?**

A  The amount of sunlight in a region

B  The movement of air masses

C  Water that falls from the sky as rain, snow, sleet, or hail

D  The increase in temperatures due to climate change

**12.** **Which term describes a long period with no rain that can lead to water shortages?**

A  Heatwave

B  Flood

C  Drought

D  Monsoon

**13.** What is meant by "climate change"?

A   Variations in weather conditions

B   A brief period of heavy rainfall

C   Changes in water temperature and extreme weather conditions

D   Long-term changes in temperature, precipitation, and other atmospheric conditions

**14.** Why are tropical regions described as having two main seasons?

A   Because they experience four distinct seasons like temperate regions.

B   Because they are located near the poles and have long winters.

C   Because they have consistently warm temperatures with wet and dry seasons.

D   Because they receive very little rain and have hot days and cool nights.

**15.** How does climate change affect the intensity of hurricanes?

A   By warming ocean temperatures, making hurricanes stronger.

B   By increasing the frequency of tropical cyclones.

C   By increasing the movement of air masses.

D   By reducing the amount of precipitation during storms.

**16.** How might increased rainfall due to climate change impact agricultural practices in tropical regions?

A   Farmers will need to shift to growing crops that require less water.

B   Farmers will rely more on artificial irrigation systems.

C   Farmers will experience longer periods of drought.

D   Farmers will need to find ways to store excess water for dry seasons.

**17.** What are some potential long-term effects of recurring heatwaves on urban areas?

- (A) Increased demand for cooling systems and air conditioning.
- (B) Increased risk of heat-related illnesses and strain on healthcare systems.
- (C) Reduction in the number of vehicles on the road due to warmer temperatures.
- (D) More frequent hurricanes disrupt city life.

**18.** How can studying weather patterns help communities prepare for climate change?

- (A) By allowing them to predict the exact date of natural disasters.
- (B) By helping them develop strategies to reduce greenhouse gas emissions.
- (C) By enabling them to construct buildings that can withstand any weather event.
- (D) By informing them about potential future weather conditions and extreme events.

**19.** Imagine you are a city planner in a coastal city. Based on your understanding of weather patterns and climate change, which of the following comprehensive plans would best help your city prepare for future extreme weather events

- (A) Constructing more high-rise buildings to accommodate population growth.
- (B) Developing a detailed emergency evacuation plan, building sea walls, and investing in flood-resistant infrastructure.
- (C) Creating an emergency response plan, building sea walls, and investing in resilient infrastructure.
- (D) Increasing the use of fossil fuels to ensure a reliable energy supply during storms.

**20.** Consider the following weather events: a heatwave in Europe and severe flooding in South Asia. Explain how climate change might have contributed to each of these events. In your response, describe one way each community can prepare for these extreme weather events in the future.

_____

_____

_____

_____

### The Tale of the Tortoise

In the dawn's gentle glow, a tortoise emerges,
A living stone, carving a slow path through the world.
His shell, a fortress of ancient secrets,
Hums with the whisper of countless seasons.

He moves like a river, slow but unyielding,
Each step a quiet drumbeat in the symphony of the forest.
Leaves flutter and murmur, applauding his passage,
As he navigates the labyrinth of roots and shadows.

A tortoise's pace, a silent meditation,
Like the hands of a clock ticking softly through time.
His eyes, windows to an ancient wisdom,
Glimmer-like stars reflected in still water.

In the pond, he is a gentle ripple,
A living paradox of strength and serenity.
The frogs croak in chorus, a percussive rhythm,
Celebrating his journey with every leap and splash.

Around him, the world is a canvas,
Painted with the hues of dawn and dusk.
The tortoise, a brushstroke of quiet persistence,
Weaves through the tapestry of life, unnoticed yet essential.

His shell, a mosaic of moss and memory,
Tells tales of the earth, whispered to the wind.
A silent philosopher, he teaches us patience,
His slow crawl a testament to enduring grace.

In the cool embrace of night, under a velvet sky, He finds
solace in the constellations' silent song. The tortoise, an
ancient voyager,
Travels through time with a heart of still waters.

21. **Which poetic device is used in the line "His shell, a fortress of ancient secrets"?**

- (A) Simile
- (B) Metaphor
- (C) Onomatopoeia
- (D) Alliteration

22. **What literary device is illustrated by the phrase "a living stone, carving a slow path through the world"?**

- (A) Metaphor
- (B) Simile
- (C) Alliteration
- (D) Onomatopoeia

23. **In the line "Leaves flutter and murmur, applauding his passage," which poetic device is being used?**

- (A) Simile
- (B) Onomatopoeia
- (C) Metaphor
- (D) Alliteration

24. **What is the main idea of the poem "The Tale of the Tortoise"?**

- (A) The tortoise's journey shows his strength.
- (B) The tortoise is a patient and wise animal.
- (C) The tortoise's journey through the forest is filled with danger.
- (D) The tortoise's slow journey represents patience and wisdom.

**25** How does the author convey the tortoise's movement in the poem?

    A    By describing the tortoise as moving slowly but with determination.

    B    By explaining that the tortoise is always late to his destinations.

    C    By comparing the tortoise's movement to the whispers of the wind.

    D    By stating that the tortoise's movements are gentle and purposeful.

**26.** In what way does the tortoise's interaction with the environment reflect the poem's message about life and nature?

    A    The tortoise's slow movement through the forest signifies the importance of taking time to appreciate life's journey.

    B    The tortoise's interactions with the forest animals show his need for companionship.

    C    The tortoise's slow journey contrasts with the fast-paced lives of other creatures and humans.

    D    The tortoise's careful navigation through the forest emphasizes the importance of mindfulness.

**27.** What can be inferred about the tortoise's perspective on life from the line "A silent philosopher, he teaches us patience"?

    A    The tortoise believes that life is best lived with restraint.

    B    The tortoise values the wisdom that comes from experiencing life at a slower pace.

    C    The tortoise thinks that life is about thinking about all aspects of oneself.

    D    The tortoise feels isolated from the other animals in the forest.

**28.** Explain how the tortoise's journey in the poem "The Tale of the Tortoise" symbolizes the themes of patience and wisdom. Relate this symbolism to a real-life situation where patience and wisdom are important. Use specific examples from the poem to support your explanation.

_____

_____

_____

_____

_____

_____

_____

_____

_____

_____

**29.** Explain how the use of the metaphor "a living stone" in the poem "The Tale of the Tortoise" helps to describe the tortoise. Provide specific examples from the poem to support your answer.

_____

_____

_____

_____

_____

_____

_____

_____

_____

_____

**30.** Analyze how the theme of the poem "The Tale of the Tortoise" can be applied to a real-life situation involving long-term goals. Use specific examples from the poem and relate them to achieving a goal over time.

_____

_____

_____

_____

_____

_____

_____

_____

_____

_____

_____

_____

_____

_____

_____

## The Skeletal System and Muscles

The skeletal system is the framework of bones that supports our bodies. It gives our body shape, protects our internal organs, and allows us to move. The human skeleton is made up of 206 bones, which are connected by joints. Bones are hard and rigid structures that store minerals like calcium and produce blood cells in the bone marrow. Muscles are soft tissues attached to bones that enable movement by contracting and relaxing. There are three types of muscles: skeletal muscles, which are connected to bones and help in movement; smooth muscles, which are found in organs and assist in functions like digestion; and cardiac muscles, which are located only in the heart and pump blood throughout the body. Together, the skeletal system and muscles work to provide support, protection, and movement, essential for the body's functionality.

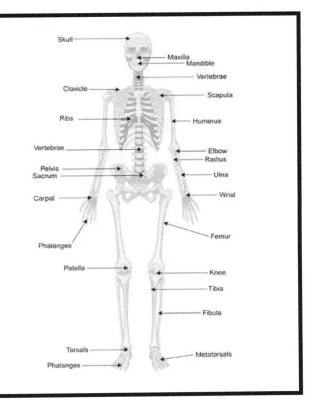

## Plant Stems and Leaves

Plant stems provide support and structure to plants, holding them upright and enabling them to reach sunlight. Stems also transport water, nutrients, and food between the roots and the leaves. Inside the stem, there are different tissues, including the xylem and phloem. The xylem carries water and minerals from the roots to the leaves, while the phloem distributes the food produced by the leaves to the rest of the plant. Plant leaves are essential for photosynthesis, the process by which plants make their own food. Leaves contain chlorophyll, a green pigment that captures sunlight, and have tiny openings called stomata that allow for gas exchange—taking in carbon dioxide and releasing oxygen. Both plant stems and leaves play crucial roles in supporting the plant and enabling it to grow and thrive.

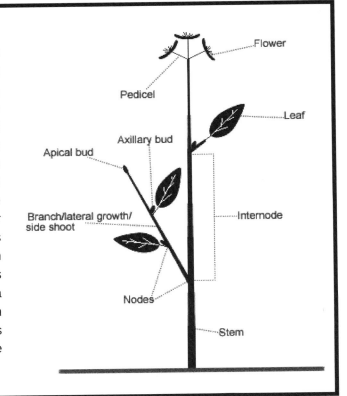

**31.** Which statement best explains the main function of the skeletal system and plant stems?

( A ) Both the skeletal system and plant stems produce food for the organism.

( B ) Both the skeletal system and plant stems provide support and structure to the organism.

( C ) Both the skeletal system and plant stems are involved in reproduction.

( D ) Both the skeletal system and plant stems store energy for the organism.

**32.** How do muscles in the human body compare to leaves in plants?

( A ) Muscles and leaves both provide support to the organism.

( B ) Muscles and leaves both help in the transportation of water and nutrients.

( C ) Muscles allow movement in the human body, while leaves perform photosynthesis in plants.

( D ) Muscles and leaves both produce blood cells for the organism.

**33.** What is a common feature of both the skeletal system and plant stem?

( A ) They both contain chlorophyll.

( B ) They both protect internal organs.

( C ) They both assist in movement.

( D ) They both provide a framework for the organism's body.

**34.** How might damage to the skeletal system in humans be similar to damage to the stems in plants?

( A ) Both could result in the organism being unable to reproduce.

( B ) Both could hinder the organism's ability to transport nutrients effectively.

( C ) Both could impair the organism's ability to store energy.

( D ) Both could lead to difficulties in movement and structural support.

**35.** Why are both the muscular system in humans and leaves in plants essential for their survival, considering their specific functions?

- (A) Both systems are involved in the respiratory processes of the organism.

- (B) Both systems enable the organism to produce and store energy.

- (C) Both systems facilitate vital processes: muscles enable movement, and leaves perform photosynthesis.

- (D) Both systems protect the organism from external damage and disease.

**36.** What are the names of the two main tissues found in plant stems that help in transporting water and nutrients?

_____

_____

_____

_____

_____

_____

_____

**37.** Describe one way in which the human skeletal system and plant stem both contribute to the protection of the organism.

_____

_____

_____

_____

_____

_____

**38.** How do the functions of muscles in humans and leaves in plants demonstrate the importance of specialized structures in living organisms?

_____

_____

_____

_____

_____

_____

_____

**39.** Evaluate the impact of technological advancements on addressing issues related to the skeletal system in humans and the vascular system in plants. Provide examples and discuss how these advancements have improved health and survival.

_____

_____

_____

_____

_____

_____

_____

**40.** Explain how the skeletal system in humans and the vascular system in plants each contribute to the movement and overall health of the organism. Use specific examples to describe what happens when each system is damaged.

_____

_____

_____

_____

_____

_____

_____

_____

_____

_____

_____

_____

_____

_____

_____

### The Secret of Willow Creek

Emily and Jacob, best friends since kindergarten, were spending their summer break in the small town of Willow Creek. Known for its peaceful surroundings and friendly community, Willow Creek was the perfect place for outdoor adventures. This summer, however, something unusual was afoot.

"Did you hear about the old mill?" Emily asked Jacob as they rode their bikes towards the creek.

"Yeah, they say it's going to be torn down," Jacob replied. "But I overheard my dad saying there's something strange about it."

Curiosity piqued, they decided to investigate. The old mill, standing tall with its weathered wooden beams and creaky floors, had been abandoned for years. It was said to be haunted, but Emily and Jacob didn't believe in ghosts. They were more interested in the stories about hidden treasures left behind by the mill's original owner, Mr. Thompson, who disappeared mysteriously decades ago.

When they reached the mill, they carefully pushed open the heavy door, which groaned in protest. Inside, dust motes danced in the sunlight filtering through broken windows. They began to explore, looking for any clues that might lead to the hidden treasure.

"Look at this," Jacob called out, pointing to a faded map pinned to the wall. It showed the layout of the mill, with a peculiar 'X' marked in the basement.

"Let's check it out," Emily said, her excitement growing.

They found the stairs leading down to the basement, each step creaking under their weight. In the dim light, they saw old machinery and stacks of wooden crates. The map led them to a corner where a loose brick caught Jacob's eye.

"Help me move this," he said.

Together, they pried the brick loose, revealing a small, hidden compartment. Inside, they found an old journal wrapped in cloth. Emily carefully opened it, revealing pages filled with Mr. Thompson's neat handwriting.

"These are his notes," Emily whispered. "He talks about discovering something valuable hidden in the creek behind the mill."

Determined to find the treasure, they made their way to the creek. The water babbled softly, and the surrounding woods were alive with the sounds of nature. They searched along the creek bank, looking for any sign of the hidden treasure.

After an hour of searching, Jacob's foot struck something hard buried in the mud. They dug around it and uncovered a small, rusted metal box. With great effort, they pried it open, revealing a collection of old coins, a locket, and a faded photograph of a young couple—Mr. Thompson and his wife.

"This must be the treasure," Emily said, her eyes wide with amazement. "But why did he hide it here?"

Jacob shrugged. "Maybe he wanted to keep it safe. Or maybe there's more to the story than we know."

As they walked back to town with their discovery, they couldn't help but feel a sense of accomplishment. They had uncovered a piece of Willow Creek's history and solved a mystery that had puzzled the town for years.

But as they shared their findings with the local historian, Mrs. Jenkins, she revealed another layer to the story. "Mr. Thompson disappeared because he was accused of stealing these coins from the town's bank. He always claimed he was innocent, but no one believed him."

Emily and Jacob exchanged glances, realizing they held the key to clearing Mr. Thompson's name. The photograph and the locket, which contained a note from Mr. Thompson's wife, proved he was away on a trip when the robbery occurred.

That night, they presented their evidence to the town council. The council members, moved by the new information, decided to reopen the case. The truth was finally revealed: Mr. Thompson had been framed by a jealous rival.

Willow Creek celebrated the newfound justice, and Emily and Jacob became local heroes. Yet, as they stood by the creek where they had discovered the box, they couldn't help but wonder—was there more to Mr. Thompson's story, or had they truly uncovered all its secrets? The possibilities were endless, and their summer adventure was one they would never forget.

**41. What motivated Emily and Jacob to investigate the old mill?**

- A) They heard it was going to be renovated.
- B) They wanted to play in the old machinery.
- C) They were curious about the hidden treasures and strange stories.
- D) They thought the mill was a good place to hide.

**42. Which clue led Emily and Jacob to find the hidden treasure?**

- A) A loose floorboard in the main room
- B) A hint from Mrs. Jenkins, the local historian
- C) The old journal found in the basement
- D) A faded map in the basement

**43. What role did the photograph and the locket play in the story?**

- A) A loose floorboard in the main room
- B) A hint from Mrs. Jenkins, the local historian
- C) The old journal found in the basement
- D) A faded map in the basement

**44.** What did Emily and Jacob find in the old mill's hidden compartment?

- (A) A treasure map
- (B) A collection of old letters
- (C) A dusty journal
- (D) A golden key

**45.** Who was the original owner of the mill mentioned in the story?

- (A) Mrs. Jenkins
- (B) Mr. Thompson
- (C) Mr. Blackwood
- (D) Eliza

**46.** Why did Emily and Jacob decide to visit the old mill?

- (A) To play with the old machinery
- (B) To look for hidden treasures and investigate strange stories
- (C) To meet Mr. Thompson
- (D) To help with its renovation

**47.** How did the old journal help Emily and Jacob in their investigation?

- (A) t provided a map of the treasure
- (B) It contained notes about the mill's history
- (C) It revealed clues about Mr. Thompson's fate and the hidden treasure
- (D) It listed names of past mill workers

**48.** Based on the clues in the story, what can be inferred about Mr. Thompson's reasons for hiding the treasure in the creek? Explain your reasoning.

A) He wanted to protect it from thieves.

B) He planned to retrieve it later.

C) He was framed and wanted to leave evidence behind.

D) He hid it as a game for future generations.

**49.** Explain how the discovery of the journal influenced Emily and Jacob's actions. Use details from the story to support your answer.

_____

_____

_____

_____

_____

_____

_____

**50.** Discuss how Emily and Jacob's investigation skills evolved throughout the story. Provide examples of how they used clues to solve the mystery.

_____

_____

_____

_____

_____

_____

**51.** Using clues from the story "The Secret of Willow Creek," write an alternate ending where Emily and Jacob discover a different outcome about Mr. Thompson's fate and the hidden treasure. Use evidence from the story to support your new ending.

_____

_____

_____

_____

_____

_____

_____

_____

_____

_____

_____

_____

_____

_____

_____

_____

_____

# Answers Test Practice 2

1. B. Uninhabited and left behind
2. C. Her strong resolve to help her community
3. A. Grief
4. A. General Sherman
5. D. She was inspired by Abigail's bravery.
6. D. They connected the past struggles to their own experiences.
7. B. The stories in Abigail's journal motivated the community to rebuild and strengthen their town.
8. A. Clara was inspired by Abigail's courage, leading her to take initiative in rebuilding her community.
9. B. Students could be inspired to form groups to identify and tackle local issues, demonstrating leadership and teamwork.
10. C. The word "resilience" highlights the townspeople's strength and ability to overcome difficulties.
11. C. Water that falls from the sky as rain, snow, sleet, or hail
12. C. Drought
13. D. Long-term changes in temperature, precipitation, and other atmospheric conditions
14. C. Because they have consistently warm temperatures with wet and dry seasons.
15. A. By warming ocean temperatures, making hurricanes stronger.
16. D. Farmers will need to find ways to store excess water for dry seasons.
17. B. Increased risk of heat-related illnesses and strain on healthcare systems.
18. D. By informing them about potential future weather conditions and extreme events.
19. B. Developing a detailed emergency evacuation plan, building sea walls, and investing in flood-resistant infrastructure.
20. **Heatwave in Europe:**
Climate change contributes to heatwaves by increasing global temperatures, leading to more frequent and intense periods of extreme heat. One way the community can prepare for heatwaves is by creating cooling centers where people can go to stay cool during extreme heat.
**Severe Flooding in South Asia:**
Climate change contributes to severe flooding by causing more intense and unpredictable rainfall patterns. One way the community can prepare for flooding is by improving drainage systems to handle heavy rain and prevent water from accumulating in residential areas.
21. B. Metaphor
22. B. Metaphor
23. B. Onomatopoeia
24. D. The turtle's slow journey represents patience and wisdom.
25. A. By describing the turtle as moving slowly but with determination.
26. A. The tortoise's slow movement through the forest signifies the importance of taking time to appreciate life's journey.
27. B. The tortoise values the wisdom that comes from experiencing life at a slower pace.
28. The tortoise's journey in the poem "The Tale of the Tortoise" symbolizes the themes of patience and wisdom in a way that can be related to real-life situations where these qualities are essential. In the poem, the tortoise moves "slow but unyielding," showing that he is patient and deliberate. This is similar to studying for a difficult exam in school. Just like the tortoise, a student must be patient and take their time to understand the material fully, rather than rushing through it.
The poem also describes the tortoise's shell as "a fortress of ancient secrets," symbolizing the wisdom he has gained over time. This can be related to the wisdom a person gains through life experiences. For example, an older person might use their life experiences to give advice to younger people, just as the tortoise's wisdom can teach others about the importance of moving thoughtfully through life.
Additionally, the tortoise's slow journey can be compared to the process of building a skill, such as learning to play a musical instrument. It takes patience to practice regularly and improve over time. The tortoise's "silent philosopher" role in the poem emphasizes that wisdom often comes from taking the time to reflect and learn, rather than rushing ahead.
In real life, just as the tortoise's steady pace allows him to navigate the forest carefully, a person who is patient and takes the time to understand their path will likely make wiser decisions. The poem teaches us that, whether it's in studying, gaining life experience, or building a skill, patience, and wisdom go hand in hand, leading to more meaningful and successful outcomes.
29. n/a
30. n/a
31. B. Both the skeletal system and plant stems provide support and structure to the organism.
32. C. Muscles allow movement in the human body, while leaves perform photosynthesis in plants.
33. D. They both provide a framework for the organism's body.
34. D. Both could lead to difficulties in movement and structural support.
35. C. Both systems facilitate vital processes: muscles enable movement, and leaves perform photosynthesis.
36. Xylem, Phloem
37. The human skeletal system protects vital internal organs, such as the brain (skull) and heart (rib cage).
Plant stems elevate leaves and flowers away from ground-level hazards, helping to protect them from damage.
38. Muscles in humans are specialized for movement, allowing the body to perform various physical activities and tasks essential for survival.
Leaves in plants are specialized for photosynthesis, capturing sunlight and converting it into food, which is vital for the plant's growth and energy needs.
39. Technological advancements in medicine, such as the development of prosthetics and joint replacements, have greatly improved the mobility and quality of life for individuals with skeletal issues, enabling them to lead more active and independent lives.
In agriculture, innovations like drip irrigation systems and advanced fertilizers have enhanced the efficiency of the vascular system in plants, ensuring optimal water and nutrient delivery, which supports healthier and more robust plant growth, leading to higher crop yields and better food security.
40. **Explanation of Functions:**
- Skeletal System:
  - Provides structure and support, enabling movement when working with muscles.
  - Protects vital organs, such as the brain and heart.
  - Stores minerals and produces blood cells.
- Vascular System in Plants:
  - Xylem transports water and minerals from the roots to the leaves.
  - The phloem distributes the food produced by photosynthesis throughout the plant.
  - Provides support to help the plant stay upright.
  Impact of Damage:

- ● **Vascular System in Plants:**
  - ○ Xylem transports water and minerals from the roots to the leaves.
  - ○ The phloem distributes the food produced by photosynthesis
  - ○ throughout the plant.
  - ○ Provides support to help the plant stay upright.

**Impact of Damage:**
- ● **Skeletal System:**
  - ○ Damage (e.g., broken bone) can impair movement, reduce protection
  - ○ for organs, and affect the production of blood cells.
  - ○ Example: A broken leg can prevent a person from walking and make
  - ○ them more vulnerable to further injury.
- ● **Vascular System in Plants:**
  - ○ Damage (e.g., broken stem) can interrupt the transport of water and nutrients, affecting the plant's ability to grow and stay healthy.
  - ○ Example: A damaged stem can cause a plant to wilt and stop
  - ○ growing due to lack of nutrients and water.

41. C. They were curious about the hidden treasures and strange stories.
42. D. A faded map in the basement
43. B. They provided evidence that Mr. Thompson was innocent.
44. C. A dusty journal
45. B. Mr. Thompson
46. B. To look for hidden treasures and investigate strange stories
47. C. It revealed clues about Mr. Thompson's fate and the hidden treasure
48. C. He was framed and wanted to leave evidence behind.
49. The discovery of the journal significantly influenced Emily and Jacob's actions by providing them with crucial information about Mr. Thompson's research and the location of the hidden treasure. The journal contained Mr. Thompson's notes, which mentioned a valuable discovery hidden in the creek behind the mill. Motivated by this information, Emily and Jacob decided to search the creek, leading to their finding the small, rusted metal box with coins, a locket, and a photograph. This discovery not only solved the mystery of the hidden treasure but also played a key role in clearing Mr. Thompson's name.
50. Emily and Jacob's investigation skills evolved significantly throughout the story. Initially, their curiosity was sparked by rumors and their desire for adventure. They started by exploring the old mill, where they found a faded map with an 'X' marked in the basement, indicating a hidden compartment. Their critical thinking skills were evident when they discovered the loose brick and found the journal.

As they read through Mr. Thompson's notes in the journal, they showed careful analysis by understanding the significance of his research and the clues pointing to the creek. They demonstrated problem-solving skills when they searched the creek bank, ultimately discovering the metal box with the hidden treasure.

Moreover, their ability to piece together historical information and personal artifacts, such as the photograph and the locket, showcased their growing investigative abilities. By presenting this evidence to the town council and confronting Mr. Blackwood, they not only solved the mystery but also helped to clear Mr. Thompson's name, showing their evolved skills in reasoning and justice.

51. **Understanding and Use of Story Clues (2 marks)**
   - ○ 2 marks: The essay effectively uses multiple clues from the story to support the new ending.
   - ○ 1 mark: The essay uses some clues from the story, but they are not fully developed or relevant.
   - ○ 0 marks: The essay does not use clues from the story or the clues are irrelevant.

**Creativity and Originality (2 marks)**
   - ○ 2 marks: The alternate ending is highly creative and original, showing a deep engagement with the story.
   - ○ 1 mark: The alternate ending shows some creativity and originality, but it may rely on common or predictable elements.
   - ○ 0 marks: The alternate ending lacks creativity and originality, or it closely mirrors the original ending.

**Coherence and Organization (2 marks)**
   - ○ 2 marks: The essay is well-organized and coherent, with a clear beginning, middle, and end that logically follows from the story.
   - ○ 1 mark: The essay is somewhat organized and coherent, but there are minor issues with the flow or structure.
   - ○ 0 marks: The essay is poorly organized or lacks coherence, making it difficult to follow.

**Grammar, Spelling, and Punctuation (1 mark)**
   - ○ 1 mark: The essay has minimal grammatical, spelling, or punctuation errors.
   - ○ 0 marks: The essay has frequent grammatical, spelling, or punctuation errors that interfere with readability.

# PRACTICE TEST 3

GET STARTED →

**Read the information text and answer items 1 - 10.**

### Discovering Alaska: A Journey Through Time and Terrain

Alaska, the largest state in the United States, is a land of vast wilderness, rich history, and diverse cultures. Situated in the far northwest of North America, this majestic region is known for its breathtaking landscapes, extreme weather conditions, and vibrant communities. From its indigenous heritage to modern-day developments, Alaska offers a unique blend of the past and the present. The state boasts a diverse topography that includes towering mountain ranges, expansive tundras, dense forests, and thousands of miles of coastline. The Alaska Range is home to Denali, the highest peak in North America, at 6,190 meters. The state's numerous glaciers, such as those in Glacier Bay National Park, provide a glimpse into the Earth's glacial history. Rivers like the Yukon and the Copper River weave through the land, supporting a variety of wildlife and ecosystems.

The weather is as varied as the landscape. The state experiences long, harsh winters and short, mild summers. In the northern regions, such as Barrow, winter temperatures can plummet to -30°C, and the sun does not rise for 65 days in the winter. Conversely, during the summer, the sun remains above the horizon for 84 days, creating the phenomenon known as the Midnight Sun. The southern coastal areas, including cities like Juneau and Ketchikan, have a more temperate maritime climate, with milder winters and abundant yearly rainfall. The culture of Alaska is a rich tapestry woven from the traditions of its indigenous peoples and the influences of various waves of settlers. Native Alaskan cultures, including the Inupiat, Yupik, Aleut, Tlingit, Haida, and Athabaskan, have thrived in the region for thousands of years. These communities have a deep connection to the land, with traditions in hunting, fishing, and storytelling that continue to this day.

Russian explorers and fur traders were among the first Europeans to arrive in the 18th century, leaving a lasting impact on the region. The United States purchased Alaska from Russia in 1867, a transaction known as "Seward's Folly," which was initially met with skepticism but later proved incredibly valuable due to the discovery of gold and oil. Modern Alaskan culture is a blend of these historical influences and contemporary American life. The state's population is diverse, with people from various ethnic backgrounds contributing to its cultural mosaic. Festivals, art, and music reflect this diversity, celebrating both indigenous heritage and modern innovation. Over the centuries, Alaska has undergone significant changes. The Klondike Gold Rush of the late 19th century brought a surge of settlers, leading to the establishment of towns and infrastructure. The construction of the Alaska Highway during World War II connected the state to the rest of the United States, facilitating further development and migration.

The discovery of oil in Prudhoe Bay in 1968 marked another turning point. The subsequent construction of the Trans-Alaska Pipeline System brought economic prosperity and transformed the state's economy. However, these developments also brought environmental and social challenges, leading to increased efforts in conservation and sustainable practices. In recent years, climate change has become a critical issue for Alaska. Rising temperatures and melting ice are impacting the state's ecosystems and the livelihoods of its people. Efforts to address these challenges are underway, with initiatives focused on renewable energy, wildlife conservation, and preserving indigenous ways of life. Alaska is a state of contrasts, where ancient traditions meet modern advancements, and serene landscapes coexist with bustling communities. Its history is a testament to resilience and adaptation, shaped by natural forces and human endeavors. As Alaska continues to evolve, it remains a place of unparalleled beauty and cultural richness, inviting all who visit or live there to appreciate its unique charm and profound significance.

1. **What is the highest peak in North America, located in Alaska?**

   (A) Mount Everest

   (B) Denali

   (C) Mount Kilimanjaro

   (D) Mount McKinley

2. **Which event in Alaska's history brought a significant increase in settlers and led to the establishment of towns and infrastructure?**

   (A) The discovery of oil in Prudhoe Bay

   (B) The purchase of Alaska from Russia

   (C) The Klondike Gold Rush

   (D) The construction of the Trans-Alaska Pipeline System

3. **How did the construction of the Alaska Highway during World War II impact Alaska?**

   (A) It led to the discovery of oil in Prudhoe Bay.

   (B) It facilitated the connection of Alaska to the rest of the United States, leading to further development and migration.

   (C) It caused significant environmental and social challenges.

   (D) It was primarily used for the transport of gold during the Klondike Gold Rush.

4. **Why was the purchase of Alaska from Russia initially met with skepticism?**

   (A) It was considered too far from the rest of the United States to be valuable.

   (B) The indigenous peoples were resistant to new settlers.

   (C) The harsh weather conditions made it uninhabitable.

   (D) The transaction was thought to be too expensive for a region with no known resources.

**5.** What does the term "Midnight Sun" refer to in the context of Alaska?

- (A) The phenomenon where the sun does not rise for 65 days in the winter.
- (B) The long, harsh winters experienced in the northern regions.
- (C) The period during summer months when the sun remains above the horizon for 84 days.
- (D) The short, mild summers in the southern coastal areas.

**6.** How have recent environmental challenges influenced efforts in Alaska to preserve its natural and cultural heritage?

- (A) Rising temperatures have led to the construction of more highways and pipelines.
- (B) Melting ice has increased the focus on renewable energy and wildlife conservation initiatives.
- (C) Increased rainfall has caused the southern coastal areas to become uninhabitable.
- (D) The discovery of more oil reserves has diminished the importance of indigenous traditions.

**7.** Describe the impact of the Klondike Gold Rush on Alaska's development. Provide specific details from the text to support your answer.

_____

_____

_____

_____

_____

_____

_____

_____

_____

_____

8. Describe two significant historical events that have shaped the development of Alaska. Explain how each event impacted the state.

_____

_____

_____

_____

_____

_____

_____

_____

9. Analyze how climate change has affected Alaska's ecosystems and the livelihood of its people. Provide specific examples from the text to support your response

_____

_____

_____

_____

_____

_____

_____

_____

**10.** Explain how the blend of indigenous traditions and modern American influences has shaped the cultural identity of Alaska. Provide specific examples from the text to support your response.

_____

_____

_____

_____

_____

_____

_____

_____

_____

_____

_____

_____

_____

_____

_____

_____

## A Bond Forged on the Court

The sun dipped below the horizon, casting long shadows over the basketball court where Ethan and Liam spent countless afternoons. The summer of 1992 had been their last before starting middle school, a time when the world seemed vast and full of endless possibilities. Their bond was forged in the heat of competition, and no one exemplified their aspirations better than Michael Jordan, the man who dominated the NBA and embodied the spirit of determination and friendship.

Ethan and Liam met in the fourth grade. Ethan had moved from another state, and Liam was the first to welcome him. Their mutual love for basketball brought them together, and soon they were inseparable. They idolized Michael Jordan, watching every game they could and emulating his moves on their local court. For them, Jordan wasn't just a basketball player; he was their idol.

Every day after school, they raced to the court, the sound of bouncing basketballs echoing through the neighborhood. They practiced layups, free throws, and their favorite – the slam dunk, though neither was quite tall enough. Ethan's mother often had to drag them home as twilight painted the sky, their laughter and shouts lingering in the evening air.

One sweltering afternoon, they decided to host a small tournament. It was nothing grand, just a few neighborhood kids coming together to play. The court was their arena, and they were determined to show their skills. Ethan and Liam were on the same team, naturally, their coordination and understanding of each other's moves were honed by years of practice.

The game was intense. Sweat dripped down their faces as they darted around, passing the ball and executing plays with the precision of their idol. As the sun climbed higher, their energy seemed to wane. But with Liam's encouragement and Ethan's relentless determination, they kept pushing forward. They remembered how Michael Jordan played through sickness in the famous "Flu Game" during the 1997 NBA Finals, showing that perseverance was key to success.

In the final moments of the game, their team was down by one point. Liam had the ball and was dribbling up the court. Ethan, sensing the opportunity, sprinted towards the basket. The seconds ticked away, and with a quick pass from Liam, Ethan leapt, his eyes focused solely on the hoop. For a moment, time seemed to stand still. The ball left his hands and soared through the air, perfectly arcing into the net as the buzzer sounded.

Their team erupted in cheers, and Liam tackled Ethan in a joyous hug. They had done it – they had won their little tournament, their small tribute to Michael Jordan's greatness. The other kids clapped them on the back.

As they sat on the bench, catching their breath, Liam turned to Ethan, a grin spreading across his face. "We did it, just like Jordan," he said, his eyes sparkling with excitement.

Ethan nodded, feeling a sense of accomplishment and gratitude for his friend. "Yeah, we did," he replied. "And we did it together."

Years later, as they watched a documentary on Jordan's career, Ethan turned to Liam. "Remember our tournament back in '92?" he asked.

Liam laughed. "How could I forget? It was the day we became champions in our own right."

**11.** **What inspired Ethan and Liam to practice basketball and host their own tournament?**

A) Their love for playing basketball.

B) Their admiration for Michael Jordan.

C) Their desire to become basketball players one day.

D) To spend more time together as friends.

**12.** **What does the word "perseverance" mean in the context of the text?**

A) Diligence in doing something despite difficulty

B) Determination to complete a task without any challenge

C) Endurance to continue an activity over a long period

D) Stubbornness in not changing one's mind

**13.** **Why was the victory in their small tournament significant to Ethan and Liam?**

A) It proved they were the best players in the neighborhood.

B) It was their first time playing together in a tournament.

C) It symbolized their strong friendship and teamwork.

D) It helped build community spirit.

**14.** **How does the text demonstrate the impact of Michael Jordan on Ethan and Liam's friendship?**

A) By illustrating how his perseverance and teamwork inspired their efforts and victories.

B) By explaining how they watched every game together which inspired them to be better basketball players.

C) By showing how they dressed like him.

D) He was the main reason they became friends in the first place.

**15.** How does the use of the word "arena" to describe the basketball court help convey the boys' feelings about the game?

( A ) Their love for playing basketball.

( B ) Their admiration for Michael Jordan.

( C ) Their desire to become basketball players one day.

( D ) To spend more time together as friends.

**16.** How do Ethan and Liam's actions and attitudes throughout the story reflect the qualities they admire in Michael Jordan, and what does this reveal about their understanding of friendship and teamwork?

( A ) They only focus on winning the game, which shows that they value competition over friendship.

( B ) They argue frequently but still manage to win, indicating that teamwork is not as important as individual talent.

( C ) They support and encourage each other, demonstrating that friendship and teamwork are crucial for achieving their goals, just as Michael Jordan's perseverance and cooperation with his team inspired them.

( D ) They play separately most of the time, suggesting that they believe personal success is more important than collaborative effort.

**17.** Which character trait best describes Liam based on his actions and attitudes in the story?

( A ) Friendly

( B ) Encouraging

( C ) Sporty

( D ) Dramatic

**18.** How does Ethan show his determination during the basketball tournament? Describe one action he takes that demonstrates this quality.

_____

_____

_____

_____

_____

_____

_____

_____

_____

_____

_____

**19.** Explain how the theme of friendship is portrayed in the story. How do Ethan and Liam's interactions on the basketball court highlight this theme?

_____

_____

_____

_____

_____

_____

_____

_____

_____

_____

_____

_____

**20.** The theme of perseverance is central to the story of Ethan and Liam. Describe how this theme is developed through their experiences on the basketball court. Include specific examples from the text to support your analysis. Additionally, discuss how the theme of perseverance in their story can be related to challenges that students might face in their own lives.

_____

_____

_____

_____

_____

_____

_____

_____

_____

_____

_____

_____

_____

_____

_____

**Read the following two information texts and answer items 21 - 30.**

### The Benefits of Controlled Screen Time for Young Children

Screen time, when used thoughtfully, can be beneficial for young children's development. Educational programs and apps offer interactive experiences that promote cognitive skills, literacy, and numeracy. According to the American Academy of Pediatrics (AAP), children aged 2 to 5 can benefit from up to one hour of high-quality screen time daily. Research by the Joan Ganz Cooney Center found that educational television shows, such as "Sesame Street," significantly improve school readiness. These programs introduce concepts like letters, numbers, and social skills in an engaging format. Additionally, interactive apps can enhance fine motor skills and problem-solving abilities. Parents can use screen time as a tool for co-viewing, which encourages discussion and reinforces learning. For instance, watching a nature documentary together can spark conversations about the environment and wildlife. Therefore, balanced and supervised screen time, combined with other activities, can support a child's learning and development.

### The Drawbacks of Excessive Screen Time for Young Children

Excessive screen time can have negative effects on young children's health and development. The World Health Organization (WHO) advises that children under five should spend no more than one hour per day on screens, and less is better. Studies have shown that too much screen time can lead to issues such as reduced physical activity, which is crucial for growth and development. According to a study published in the journal Pediatrics, higher screen time is associated with delays in language development and poorer social skills. It can also interfere with sleep patterns; exposure to blue light from screens can disrupt the production of melatonin, a hormone that regulates sleep. Moreover, passive consumption of content does not provide the same cognitive and social benefits as interactive, real-world play. Young children need hands-on experiences to develop their motor skills and social interactions. Therefore, limiting screen time and encouraging more active, unstructured play is essential for the healthy growth of young children.

**21.** According to the paragraph, what is one-way parents can make screen time beneficial for young children?

A  Their love for playing basketball.

B  Their admiration for Michael Jordan.

C  Their desire to become basketball players one day.

D  To spend more time together as friends.

**22.** According to the paragraph, why is limiting screen time important for young children?

A  It ensures children have more time for interactive, real-world play.

B  It helps children become better at using digital devices.

C  It guarantees children will perform better academically enhancing their social skills.

D  It allows children to watch educational programs to prepare for school.

**23.** Based on the information in both paragraphs, which statement best summarizes the differing perspectives on screen time for young children?

A  Screen time is universally harmful to young children's development and should be avoided completely.

B  Screen time can be beneficial when used in moderation and with high-quality content, but excessive use can lead to negative effects.

C  Screen time has no impact on young children's development and can be used without any limitations to improve children's school readiness

D  Screen time should be unlimited for educational purposes, as it always enhances children's cognitive skills.

**24.** According to the text, how much screen time does the American Academy of Pediatrics (AAP) recommend for children aged 2 to 5?

A  No screen time

B  Up to one hour daily

C  Up to two hours daily

D  Unlimited screen time

**25.** Which of the following best describes an activity that parents can engage in to make screen time more beneficial for young children?

- (A) Allowing children to play video games alone

- (B) Encouraging children to watch any television shows

- (C) Co-viewing and discussing educational content

- (D) Using screen time as a reward for good behavior

**26.** Based on the texts, what is one reason why the World Health Organization (WHO) recommends limited screen time for young children?

- (A) To increase children's time spent on homework

- (B) To prevent disruptions in sleep patterns caused by blue light

- (C) To enhance children's social media skills

- (D) To promote the use of digital learning apps

**27.** Compare and contrast the views of the American Academy of Pediatrics (AAP) and the World Health Organization (WHO) on screen time for young children. What are the similarities and differences in their recommendations and reasons?

- (A) Both recommend unlimited screen time but for different reasons.

- (B) Both recommend limited screen time; the AAP for promoting education, and the WHO for avoiding physical and developmental issues.

- (C) The AAP recommends no screen time, while the WHO encourages it for educational purposes.

- (D) The AAP focuses on screen time for entertainment, and the WHO focuses on screen time for educational apps.

**28.** Using information from both paragraphs, describe two strategies parents can use to manage their young children's screen time effectively. Explain how each strategy addresses the potential benefits or drawbacks of screen time.

_____

_____

_____

_____

72

_____

_____

_____

_____

_____

_____

**29.** Using details from both texts, explain how screen time can impact a young child's sleep patterns. Provide one specific example from the text to support your explanation.

_____

_____

_____

_____

_____

_____

_____

_____

_____

_____

_____

_____

**20.** Using the information from both paragraphs on the benefits and drawbacks of screen time for young children, write an essay discussing whether you think screen time should be limited or encouraged for young children. In your essay, include the following:

An introduction that presents your main argument.

Two paragraphs to support your argument with examples from the text.

A counterargument paragraph that acknowledges the opposing view and refutes it with evidence from the text.

A conclusion that summarizes your main points and reinforces your argument.

_____

_____

_____

_____

_____

_____

_____

_____

_____

_____

_____

_____

_____

_____

Read the following poem and answer items 31 - 40.

**A Symphony of Love and Grace**

In our house of many hues,
We share our dreams and different views.
Mom with stories from the sea,
Dad with roots from an old oak tree.

Sister's songs of distant lands,
Brother's drawings with his hands.
Grandma's tales of moonlit nights,
Grandpa's wisdom, shining bright.

Around the table, laughter flows,
Love in every smile grows.
Each voice unique, a melody,
In harmony, our hearts are free.

From spicy meals to sweet delights,
Every meal, a feast of sights.
Cultures blend in perfect rhyme,
A dance of flavors, lost in time.
Through thick and thin, we stand as one,
Under moon, and under sun.

A patchwork quilt, we're stitched so tight,
A family bound by love's pure light.
In our home, the world's embraced,
Every corner, every face.
A symphony of love and grace,
In our hearts, we find our place.

**31.** Which line from the poem "A Symphony of Love and Grace" emphasizes the diversity of the family's backgrounds?

A  A patchwork quilt, we're stitched so tight,"

B  "Sister's songs of distant lands,"

C  "Love in every smile grows."

D  "In harmony, our hearts are free."

76

**32.** How does the imagery in the poem "A Symphony of Love and Grace" help convey the theme of unity in diversity?

- (A) By describing the family's meals as "a feast of sights."
- (B) By illustrating the blend of cultures as "a dance of flavors."
- (C) By depicting the family's support as "standing as one, Under moon, and under sun."
- (D) By showing the variety of contributions with "Mom with stories from the sea, Dad with roots from an old oak tree."

**33.** Which lines from the poem "A Symphony of Love and Grace" best illustrate how the family members' diverse backgrounds enrich their collective experiences?

- (A) "Around the table, laughter flows, Love in every smile grows."
- (B) "From spicy meals to sweet delights, Every meal, a feast of sights."
- (C) Through thick and thin, we stand as one, Under moon, and under sun."
- (D) "Each voice unique, a melody, In harmony, our hearts are free."

**34.** In the poem "A Symphony of Love and Grace," what is the meaning of the phrase "a patchwork quilt, we're stitched so tight"?

- (A) The family enjoys making quilts together.
- (B) The family members wear colorful clothing.
- (C) The family is closely connected despite their differences.
- (D) The family lives in a house decorated with quilts.

**35.** How does the poet use the metaphor "a symphony of love and grace" to enhance the reader's understanding of the family's dynamic in the poem "A Symphony of Love and Grace"?

- (A) By suggesting that the family members play musical instruments together.
- (B) By indicating that the family experiences both love and hardship.
- (C) By comparing the family's harmonious relationships to a well-coordinated musical performance.
- (D) By emphasizing the family's interest in music and dance.

**36.** Which lines from the poem "A Symphony of Love and Grace" best support the idea that the family's diversity contributes to a richer, more fulfilling life?

(A) "Around the table, laughter flows, Love in every smile grows."

(B) "Each voice unique, a melody, In harmony, our hearts are free."

(C) "Grandma's tales of moonlit nights, Grandpa's wisdom, shining bright."

(D) "A patchwork quilt, we're stitched so tight, A family bound by love's pure light."

**33.** How does the poet use the descriptions of family members' contributions to highlight the theme of unity in diversity in the poem "A Symphony of Love and Grace"?

(A) By showing that each family member has a unique talent that contributes to the household.

(B) By emphasizing the importance of cultural heritage through individual stories.

(C) By describing the family's varied meals and traditions in detail.

(D) By illustrating that despite their differences, the family members create a loving environment.

**38.** How does the poet's use of the dining table as a central image in "A Symphony of Love and Grace" symbolize the family's unity? Discuss the significance of this image and provide specific examples from the poem to support your answer.

_____

_____

_____

_____

_____

_____

_____

_____

39. **Discuss how the poet's portrayal of different family members in "A Symphony of Love and Grace" helps to convey the poem's theme. Analyze how the characters' unique attributes and contributions create a sense of harmony within the family. Provide specific examples from the poem to support your analysis.**

**40.** Evaluate how the poet's use of cultural references and descriptive language in "A Symphony of Love and Grace" enhances the reader's understanding of the family's diverse background. Explain how these elements contribute to the overall theme of the poem. Provide specific examples from the poem to support your answer.

_____

_____

_____

_____

_____

_____

_____

_____

_____

_____

_____

_____

_____

_____

_____

_____

**Read the following short story and answer items 41 - 51.**

---

### The Guardians of Dragonstone Mountain

In a small village nestled at the base of Dragonstone Mountain, lived a brave boy named Leo. Dragonstone Mountain was a place of mystery and legend, its towering peaks often hidden by swirling mists. The villagers believed that dragons, ancient and wise, slumbered deep within the mountain's caverns, guarding treasures and secrets long forgotten.

Leo had always been fascinated by the tales of dragons. His grandmother often recounted stories of the great dragons that once soared through the skies, their scales glinting like gold in the sunlight, their roars echoing like thunder across the land. One story, in particular, captivated Leo's imagination - the legend of the Dragon's Heart, a magical gem said to possess the power to control the elements.

One evening, as the sun dipped below the horizon, casting a golden glow over the village, Leo's grandmother fell gravely ill. The village healer shook his head sadly, unable to cure her. Desperate to save her, Leo remembered the legend of the Dragon's Heart and decided to embark on a daring quest to find it.

Armed with his courage and a map his grandmother had given him, Leo set off towards Dragonstone Mountain. The path was treacherous, filled with steep cliffs and dense forests. But Leo's determination never wavered. He climbed higher and higher, driven by love for his grandmother and the hope of finding the magical gem.

After days of arduous travel, Leo finally reached the entrance to a hidden cave, marked by ancient carvings of dragons. Taking a deep breath, he stepped inside. The cave was vast and dark, with the sound of dripping water echoing through the silence. Leo lit a torch and carefully made his way deeper into the mountain.

As he ventured further, the air grew warmer, and the walls of the cave began to shimmer with a soft, golden light. Suddenly, Leo found himself in a massive chamber, filled with glittering treasures - piles of gold, silver, and jewels beyond imagination. And there, in the center of the chamber, lay a colossal dragon, its scales gleaming like molten gold.

Leo approached the dragon cautiously. "Great dragon," he called out, his voice steady but respectful, "I seek the Dragon's Heart to save my grandmother."

The dragon's eyes slowly opened, and it regarded Leo with a mixture of curiosity and wisdom. "You are brave, young one," the dragon rumbled, its voice echoing through the chamber. "But the Dragon's Heart is not a mere gem. It is a symbol of the bond between humans and dragons, a bond forged through trust and respect."
Leo nodded, his heart pounding. "I understand. Please, teach me how to earn your trust."

For days, Leo remained in the chamber, learning from the dragon. He listened to stories of the ancient times when dragons and humans lived in harmony, and he learned the importance of balance and respect for all living beings. The dragon saw Leo's sincerity and determination, and it was moved by his selfless love for his grandmother.
Finally, the dragon granted Leo the Dragon's Heart, a radiant gem that pulsed with a warm, golden light. "Use its power wisely," the dragon advised. "Remember the lessons you have learned, and the bond we share."

With the Dragon's Heart in hand, Leo hurried back to his village. He placed the gem beside his grandmother, and its healing light enveloped her. Slowly, she opened her eyes, her strength restored.

The villagers rejoiced, and from that day on, Leo became known as the Guardian of Dragonstone Mountain. He shared the wisdom he had gained, teaching his people to live in harmony with nature and to respect the ancient bond between humans and dragons. And so, the legend of Leo and the Dragon's Heart became a timeless tale of bravery, wisdom, and the enduring power of love.

**41.** What is the primary lesson that Leo learns from the dragon during his quest?

- (A) How to communicate with animals
- (B) The importance of balance and respect for all living beings
- (C) The location of the Dragon's Heart
- (D) How to heal his grandmother

**42.** What motivates Leo to embark on his quest to Dragonstone Mountain?

- (A) His desire to become famous
- (B) His need to find hidden treasures
- (C) His love for his grandmother
- (D) His wish to meet the legendary dragon

**43.** Who is the main character in the story "The Guardians of Dragonstone Mountain"?

- (A) Leo
- (B) Elara
- (C) The Dragon
- (D) The village healer

**44.** What is Leo's primary goal in the story?

- (A) To find hidden treasure
- (B) To save his grandmother
- (C) To become a warrior
- (D) To find a dragon

**45.** Which of the following best describes the relationship between Leo and the dragon?

- (A) Hostile
- (B) respectful and instructive
- (C) Competitive
- (D) Indifferent

**46.** What motivates Leo to seek out the Dragon's Heart?

- (A) He wants to prove his bravery.
- (B) He desires wealth and power.
- (C) He hopes to cure his grandmother's illness.
- (D) He is curious about dragons.

**47.** How does the author use descriptive language to create a sense of mystery and adventure in the story? Provide an example from the text.

_____

_____

_____

_____

_____

_____

_____

_____

_____

_____

_____

_____

_____

_____

**48.** How does the author use descriptive language to create a sense of mystery and adventure in the story? Provide an example from the text.

_____

_____

_____

_____

_____

_____

_____

_____

_____

_____

_____

**49.** Evaluate the effectiveness of Leo's leadership in his village after returning from his quest. How might his new knowledge and experience impact his community in the long term?

_____

_____

_____

_____

_____

_____

_____

_____

**50.** Explain how Leo's character changes from the beginning to the end of the story. Use specific details from the text to support your response.

_____

_____

_____

_____

_____

_____

_____

_____

**51.** In the story "The Guardians of Dragonstone Mountain," identify and explain the meaning of two words that contribute to the magical and mysterious tone of the story. Use context clues from the text to support your definitions.

_____

_____

_____

_____

_____

_____

_____

_____

_____

_____

_____

_____

_____

_____

_____

_____

_____

# Answers Test Practice 3

1. B. Denali
2. C. The Klondike Gold Rush
3. B. It facilitated the connection of Alaska to the rest of the United States, leading to further development and migration.
4. D. The transaction was thought to be too expensive for a region with no known resources.
5. C. The period during summer months when the sun remains above the horizon for 84 days.
6. B. Melting ice has increased the focus on renewable energy and wildlife conservation initiatives.
7. 1 mark for identifying the Klondike Gold Rush. 1 mark for describing its impact on Alaska's development with specific details from the text.
**Example Answer:** The Klondike Gold Rush brought a significant increase in settlers to Alaska, leading to the establishment of towns and infrastructure, which facilitated further development.
8. **Rubric:** 1 mark for identifying and describing the first historical event and its impact. 1 mark for identifying and describing the second historical event and its impact.
**Example Answer:** The Klondike Gold Rush brought a surge of settlers to Alaska, leading to the establishment of towns and infrastructure. The discovery of oil in Prudhoe Bay in 1968 brought economic prosperity and transformed the state's economy through the construction of the Trans-Alaska Pipeline System.
9. 1 mark for explaining the effects of climate change on Alaska's ecosystems. 1 mark for explaining the effects on the livelihood of its people with specific examples from the text.
Example Answer: Climate change has caused rising temperatures and melting ice in Alaska, impacting ecosystems by altering habitats and threatening wildlife. This has also affected the livelihood of people who depend on these ecosystems, leading to initiatives focused on **renewable energy and wildlife conservation to address these challenges.**
10. **Rubric:** 1 mark for explaining how indigenous traditions have contributed to Alaska's cultural identity. 1 mark for explaining how modern American influences have contributed to Alaska's cultural identity and providing specific examples from the text.
**Example Answer:** Indigenous traditions, such as those of the Inupiat, Yupik, and Tlingit, have shaped Alaska's cultural identity through practices in hunting, fishing, and storytelling that remain important today. Modern American influences, such as the impact of Russian explorers and the discovery of oil, have also contributed to the state's culture by bringing diverse populations and economic developments. Festivals, art, and music in Alaska reflect this blend, celebrating both indigenous heritage and modern innovations.
11. B. Their admiration for Michael Jordan.
12. A. Diligence in doing something despite difficulty
13. C. It symbolized their strong friendship and teamwork.
14. A. By illustrating how his perseverance and teamwork inspired their efforts and victories.
15. B. It suggests that the boys saw their games as important and exciting battles.
16. C. They support and encourage each other, demonstrating that friendship and teamwork are crucial for achieving their goals, just as Michael Jordan's perseverance and cooperation with his team inspired them.
17. B. Encouraging
18. **2 Marks:** Response clearly describes how Ethan shows his determination, using a specific action from the text to illustrate this quality.
**Example Answer:** Ethan shows his determination by sprinting towards the basket in the final moments of the game and successfully scoring the winning basket despite the pressure and exhaustion.
**1 Mark:** Response describes Ethan's determination but lacks a specific action or is unclear. **Example Answer:** Ethan tries really hard to win the game.
**0 Marks:** Response does not describe Ethan's determination or provides irrelevant information. **Example Answer:** Ethan plays basketball.
19. **2 Marks:** Response provides a clear explanation of how the theme of friendship is portrayed, using specific interactions between Ethan and Liam from the text. **Example Answer:** The theme of friendship is portrayed through Ethan and Liam's teamwork and support for each other. For instance, when Liam encourages Ethan and passes him the ball in the final seconds, showing their mutual trust and cooperation.
**1 Mark:** Response explains the theme of friendship but lacks specific interactions or is unclear. **Example Answer:** The theme of friendship is shown by Ethan and Liam working together to win the game.
**0 Marks:** Response does not explain the theme of friendship or provides irrelevant information. **Example Answer:** The theme of friendship is about playing basketball.
20. **4 Marks:** Response provides a thorough and insightful analysis of how the theme of perseverance is developed through Ethan and Liam's experiences, using multiple specific examples from the text. The response also effectively relates the theme of perseverance to challenges that students might face in their own lives, demonstrating a deep understanding of the theme's relevance.
**3 Marks:** Response provides a clear analysis of how the theme of perseverance is developed through Ethan and Liam's experiences, using some specific examples from the text. The response relates the theme of perseverance to challenges that students might face in their own lives, with minor omissions or less depth.
**2 Marks:** Response provides a basic analysis of how the theme of perseverance is developed through Ethan and Liam's experiences, with limited examples from the text. The response briefly relates the theme of perseverance to challenges that students might face in their own lives but lacks detail.
**1 Mark:** Response provides a minimal analysis with few or no examples from the text. The response may touch on the theme of perseverance and its relevance to students' lives but is underdeveloped.
**0 Marks:** Response does not address the question or provides irrelevant information.
21. C. Using screen time as a tool for co-viewing and discussing educational content.
22. A. It ensures children have more time for interactive, real-world play.
23. B. Screen time can be beneficial when used in moderation and with high-quality content, but excessive use can lead to negative effects.
24. B. Up to one hour daily
25. C. Co-viewing and discussing educational content.
26. B. To prevent disruptions in sleep patterns caused by blue light.
27. B. Both recommend limited screen time; the AAP for promoting education, and the WHO for avoiding physical and developmental issues.
28. **1 mark:** The response accurately describes one strategy parents can use to manage screen time and explains how it addresses the potential benefits (e.g., co-viewing educational content to encourage learning and discussion).
**1 mark:** The response accurately describes another strategy and explains how it addresses the potential drawbacks (e.g., limiting screen time to ensure children have enough physical activity and real-world play).
29. **1 mark:** The response accurately explains how screen time can impact sleep patterns, using details from the text (e.g., exposure to blue light disrupting melatonin production).
**1 mark:** The response provides a specific example from the text to support the explanation (e.g., the World Health Organization's recommendation to limit screen time to prevent sleep disruptions).

30. **1 mark:** Introduction that clearly states the main argument.
**2 marks:** Two paragraphs that support the argument with relevant examples and details from the text.
**2 marks:** A counterargument paragraph that acknowledges the opposing view and effectively refutes it with evidence from the text.
**1 mark:** Conclusion that summarizes the main points and reinforces the argument.
**1 mark:** Overall coherence, clarity, and use of appropriate vocabulary.
31. A. "A patchwork quilt, we're stitched so tight,"
32. C. By depicting the family's support as "standing as one, Under moon, and under sun."
33. B. "From spicy meals to sweet delights, Every meal, a feast of sights."
34. C. The family is closely connected despite their differences.
35. C. By comparing the family's harmonious relationships to a well-coordinated musical performance.
36. B. "Each voice unique, a melody, In harmony, our hearts are free."
37. D. By illustrating that despite their differences, the family members create a loving environment
38. **1 mark:** Explanation of the dining table as a symbol of family unity.
**1 mark:** Specific examples from the poem to support the explanation.3
The poet uses the dining table as a central image to symbolize the family's unity by describing it as a place where "laughter flows" and "love in every smile grows." This image represents the coming together of different family members, each with their own stories and backgrounds, to share meals and experiences. The phrase "a feast of sights" signifies the diverse cultural heritage and traditions that blend together at the table, reinforcing the theme of unity in diversity.
39. **1 mark:** Analysis of how the portrayal of family members conveys the poem's theme.
**1 mark:** Specific examples from the poem to support the analysis.
The poet's portrayal of different family members conveys the theme of unity in diversity by highlighting each person's unique attributes and contributions. For example, the mother shares "stories from the sea," and the father has "roots from an old oak tree," showcasing their varied backgrounds. The sister's "songs of distant lands" and the brother's "drawings with his hands" illustrate the diverse talents within the family. Grandma's "tales of moonlit nights" and Grandpa's
"wisdom, shining bright" further emphasize the rich tapestry of experiences and knowledge. These individual traits create a harmonious and loving environment, as seen in the lines "Each voice unique, a melody, In harmony, our hearts are free," demonstrating how their differences enhance their unity.
40. **1 mark:** Evaluation of how cultural references and descriptive language enhance the understanding of the family's diversity.
**1 mark:** Specific examples from the poem to support the evaluation.
41. B. The importance of balance and respect for all living beings
42. C. His love for his grandmother
43. A. Leo
44. B. To save his grandmother
45. Respectful and instructive
46. C. He hopes to cure his grandmother's illness.
47. The author uses descriptive language to create a vivid and enchanting setting, such as "the towering peaks often hidden by swirling mists" and "the walls of the cave began to shimmer with a soft, golden light." These descriptions enhance the mysterious and adventurous atmosphere of the story.
48. The dragon serves as a mentor to Leo, teaching him valuable lessons about respect, balance, and the bond between humans and nature. Their interaction helps Leo grow from a boy driven by a singular goal to a wise guardian who
understands the importance of harmony and responsibility. This contributes to the story's theme of personal growth and the importance of wisdom and respect.
49. Leo's leadership is effective because he applies the wisdom and respect he learned from the dragon to his community. By teaching the villagers to live in harmony with nature and respect the ancient bonds, he promotes a sustainable and peaceful coexistence. In the long term, this can lead to a stronger, more united community that values and protects its environment, ensuring the well-being of future generations
50. Leo's character undergoes significant development throughout the story. At the beginning, he is portrayed as a brave but somewhat naive boy, driven by desperation to save his grandmother. His initial motivation is purely to find the Dragon's Heart, a magical gem he believes will heal her. However, as he embarks on his quest and interacts with the dragon, Leo learns valuable lessons about balance, respect, and the bond between humans and dragons. These lessons indicate a shift from a single-minded focus on his grandmother's health to a broader understanding of his role in the world. By the end of the story, Leo has transformed into a wise and respectful guardian who understands the importance of harmony between all living beings, demonstrating his growth from a brave boy to a mature and responsible young man. The dragon's trust in him and the granting of the Dragon's Heart further signify his newfound wisdom and understanding.
51. One word that contributes to the magical and mysterious tone of the story is "treacherous." In the context of Leo's journey, the path to Dragonstone Mountain is described as "treacherous," filled with steep cliffs and dense forests. This word suggests that the path is dangerous and difficult to navigate, emphasizing the perilous nature of Leo's quest and adding to the sense of adventure and uncertainty. Another word is "slumbered." The dragons are said to "slumber" within the mountain's caverns, which implies a deep, magical sleep. This word choice enhances the mythical quality of the dragons, suggesting they are ancient, powerful beings who are not merely sleeping but are in a profound state of rest, awaiting a time of need or great importance. The use of "slumbered" instead of "slept" evokes a sense of timelessness and enchantment, adding to the story's magical atmosphere.

**Read the story and answer items 1 - 10.**

### The Melody of Knowledge

In the vibrant town of Harmony Springs, music was not just a hobby—it was a way of life. Every morning, the streets came alive with the melodies of flutes, the beats of drums, and the hum of violins. It was a town where every heart had a rhythm, and every soul a song.

Among the residents was a curious and bright 12-year-old girl named Maya. She loved everything about music, from the way it made her feel to the stories it told. Maya's family had recently moved to Harmony Springs, and she was eager to learn more about the town's deep connection to music.

One sunny afternoon, Maya's teacher, Mr. Avery, took the class on a field trip to the Melody Library, a place known for its vast collection of music sheets and instruments from all over the world. As they walked through the grand entrance, Maya's eyes widened at the sight of rows and rows of ancient books, each with a unique story to tell.

Mr. Avery guided the students to a special section where the oldest music manuscripts were kept. He explained, "These manuscripts hold not just music, but the wisdom of ages. Every note, every rhythm has a story, a piece of knowledge passed down through generations."

Maya was fascinated. She carefully picked up a dusty old manuscript titled "The Symphony of Stars." As her fingers traced the faded notes, she felt a strange connection, as if the music was speaking directly to her. Mr. Avery noticed her interest and smiled. "Music," he said, "is a universal language. It can teach us about cultures, history, and even ourselves."

That evening, inspired by her visit to the Melody Library, Maya decided to create her own piece of music. She sat by her window, gazing at the stars, and began to play her violin. The notes flowed like a gentle stream, each one carrying a piece of her thoughts, dreams, and curiosities.

As she played, she imagined the stars twinkling in response, sharing their ancient secrets with her. She thought about the people who had come before her, those who had written the manuscripts in the library, and the knowledge they had passed down. Her music became a bridge, connecting the past with the present, and she felt a profound sense of belonging and understanding.

Maya's melody caught the attention of her neighbors, who gathered outside her window, enchanted by the beautiful music. Among them was Mrs. Chang, an elderly woman who had lived in Harmony Springs her entire life. She approached Maya the next day and shared a story about how music had helped her learn about her own heritage and family history.

"Music," Mrs. Chang said, "is a powerful teacher. It helps us remember who we are and where we come from. It connects us and the world around us."

Maya realized that music was more than just notes on a page—it was a vessel of knowledge, carrying lessons and stories across time and space. Inspired by this revelation, she started a project at school where students could share music from their cultures and learn about the histories and traditions behind them.

The project was a huge success. Students brought instruments, sang songs, and shared dances from their cultural backgrounds. Each performance was a lesson, teaching them about different lands, people, and ways of life. Harmony Springs became even more connected, its residents bonded by the shared knowledge that music had brought into their lives.

1. **What inspired Maya to create her piece of music in "The Melody of Knowledge"?**

   (A) A conversation with Mrs. Chang.

   (B) A lesson from Mr. Avery about ancient manuscripts.

   (C) A visit to the Melody Library.

   (D) A field trip to a concert hall.

2. **How did Maya's project at school help her classmates understand different cultures?**

   (A) By allowing students to write their music.

   (B) By encouraging students to share and perform music from their cultural backgrounds.

   (C) By having Mr. Avery teach them about ancient music manuscripts.

   (D) By organizing field trips to the Melody Library.

3. **What does Maya's experience in the story suggest about the role of music in connecting people and cultures?**

   (A) Music can help people remember their heritage and learn about others.

   (B) Music is only useful for personal enjoyment.

   (C) Music is mainly important for historical preservation.

   (D) Music can only be understood by those who play instruments.

4. **What does the word "manuscript" refer to in the context of the story?**

   (A) A modern printed book.

   (B) A handwritten or typed document.

   (C) A musical instrument.

   (D) A type of sheet music.

5. In the story, how does the use of the word "vessel" in the phrase "music was a vessel of knowledge" enhance the reader's understanding of music's role?

(A) It emphasizes that music can physically carry objects.

(B) It implies that music is fragile and easily broken.

(C) It indicates that music is an ancient tradition.

(D) It suggests that music is a container that holds and transports knowledge across time.

6. How does the story illustrate the idea that music is a universal language?

(A) By showing Maya composing a piece of music on her own.

(B) By describing the town of Harmony Springs where everyone loves music.

(C) By highlighting the project where students share music from their cultures and learn about each other's histories.

(D) By detailing Mr. Avery's lesson on ancient music manuscripts.

7. What can be inferred about the importance of music in Harmony Springs based on Maya's experiences and the community's reaction to her playing?

(A) Music is an essential part of the town's identity and daily life.

(B) Music is appreciated by the older residents of Harmony Springs.

(C) Music is considered a community activity.

(D) Music is taught in schools.

8. Which sentence from the story uses a simile to describe music?

(A) "The streets came alive with the melodies of flutes, the beats of drums, and the hum of violins."

(B) "The notes flowed like a gentle stream, each one carrying a piece of her thoughts, dreams, and curiosities."

(C) Music was a vessel of knowledge, carrying lessons and stories across time and space."

(D) "Maya's eyes widened at the sight of rows and rows of ancient books, each with a unique story to tell."

91

9. Analyze how the author uses Maya's interactions with the community to illustrate the theme of music as a unifying force. How do these interactions help Maya and her classmates understand the broader significance of music? Use specific details from the story to support your response.

_____

_____

_____

_____

_____

_____

_____

_____

_____

_____

10. Describe Maya's transformation from the beginning to the end of the story regarding her understanding and appreciation of music. How do her experiences in Harmony Springs shape her perception of music's importance in society? Provide specific examples from Maya's interactions and actions in the story to support your answer.

_____

_____

_____

_____

_____

**Read the information text and answer items 11 - 20.**

### The Impact of Technology on the Music Industry.

Over the past century, technology has dramatically transformed the music industry, shaping how music is created, distributed, and consumed. In the early 1900s, the invention of the radio brought music into homes across America, making it accessible without attending live performances. Records, made of shellac and later vinyl, allowed people to buy and listen to their favorite songs repeatedly, with musician Louis Armstrong famously saying, "What we play is life." The 1940s and 1950s introduced magnetic tape and multitrack recording, enabling more complex and polished music productions. Les Paul, an early pioneer, noted, "You can make things sound a lot more like what you hear in your head." The 1980s saw the advent of the compact disc (CD), offering superior sound quality and durability. The late 1990s revolutionized music distribution with MP3s, which compressed audio files for easy sharing and downloading. Shawn Fanning, creator of Napster, said, "I wanted to build something that would be like a library of music available to anyone at any time." Today, streaming services like Spotify, Apple Music, and YouTube are the primary ways people listen to music, providing instant access to millions of songs. Daniel Ek, co-founder of Spotify, remarked, "We want to create a service that takes the complexity out of the music experience." Modern music production relies heavily on digital audio workstations (DAWs) like Pro Tools and Logic Pro, allowing musicians to create, edit, and produce music entirely on a computer. Grammy-winning producer Quincy Jones stated, "The technology is just amazing. There are no limitations anymore." From the radio to streaming services, technology has continuously shaped the music industry, breaking down barriers and creating new opportunities for artists and listeners alike, with exciting possibilities for the future.

**11.** **What was the primary way people listened to music in the early 1900s?**

(A) CDs

(B) Radio

(C) MP3s

(D) Streaming services

**12.** Who is the creator of Napster?

- (A) Les Paul
- (B) Daniel Ek
- (C) Quincy Jones
- (D) Shawn Fanning

**13.** Which of the following technologies allowed for multitrack recording?

- (A) Magnetic Tape
- (B) Vinyl Records
- (C) Streaming services
- (D) MP3s

**14.** What innovation in the 1980s offered better sound quality and durability than vinyl records?

- (A) Radio
- (B) Compact Discs
- (C) MP3s
- (D) Streaming services

**15.** Why did MP3s revolutionize music distribution in the late 1990s?

- (A) They provided better sound quality than CDs
- (B) They allowed for multitrack recording
- (C) They made it easy to share and download music
- (D) They were the first form of digital audio

**16.** What impact did the introduction of streaming services have on the way people access music?

(A) It made music more expensive

(B) It restricted access to certain regions

(C) It provided instant access to millions of songs

(D) It increased the variety of available music

**17.** Analyze how digital audio workstations (DAWs) have influenced music production compared to earlier technologies.

(A) DAWs have allowed musicians to create, edit, and produce music entirely on a computer

(B) DAWs have increased the creativity of musicians and allowed for better collaboration

(C) DAWs have made music production slower and more difficult for musicians to understand

(D) DAWs have replaced the need for musical instruments

**18.** Compare and contrast the impact of CDs and MP3s on the music industry. Which statement is true?

(A) CDs allowed for easy sharing of music over the internet, while MP3s offered better sound quality.

(B) Both CDs and MP3s compressed audio files for easy distribution.

(C) CDs offered better sound quality and durability, while MP3s revolutionized music distribution by making it easy to share and download music over the Internet.

(D) Both CDs and MP3s made live music performances obsolete.

**19.** Explain how the invention of magnetic tape and multitrack recording in the mid-20th century changed the process of creating music. Use examples from the text to support your response.

_____

_____

_____

_____

_____

_____

_____

_____

_____

_____

_____

**20.** Evaluate the impact of streaming services on the music industry and how they have changed the way people access music. Compare this to the earlier technological advancements mentioned in the text. Provide specific details to support your answer.

_____

_____

_____

_____

_____

_____

_____

_____

_____

_____

_____

_____

**Read the two information texts and answer items 21 - 29.**

**Text 1: The African Elephant**

The African elephant is the largest land mammal on Earth. These majestic creatures are primarily found in sub-Saharan Africa, thriving in a variety of habitats, including savannas, forests, and deserts. African elephants are known for their massive bodies, large ears, and long trunks. The trunk, which is an elongated nose and upper lip, is a versatile tool used for breathing, smelling, touching, grasping, and producing sounds.

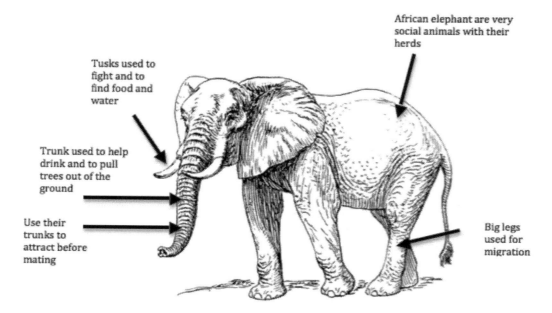

African elephant are very social animals with their herds

Tusks used to fight and to find food and water

Trunk used to help drink and to pull trees out of the ground

Use their trunks to attract before mating

Big legs used for migration

African elephants are herbivores, meaning they primarily consume plant-based food. Their diet includes leaves, bark, fruit, and grasses. An adult elephant can eat up to 300 pounds of vegetation in a single day! This diet requires them to spend about 16 hours a day feeding. Their large ears help regulate their body temperature, flapping to cool the blood that flows through their many blood vessels.

Elephants live in social groups called herds, which are usually led by the oldest female, known as the matriarch. These herds are typically made up of related females and their offspring. Male elephants, on the other hand, tend to leave the herd when they reach adolescence and may live solitary lives or form smaller bachelor groups.

One of the most fascinating aspects of African elephants is their complex social behavior and communication. They use a range of vocalizations, from trumpets to low-frequency rumbles, which can travel long distances. They also communicate through body language and touch, demonstrating strong bonds and cooperation within the herd.

Despite their impressive size and strength, African elephants face significant threats from habitat loss and poaching. They are targeted for their ivory tusks, which has led to a severe decline in their population. Conservation efforts are crucial to protect these gentle giants and ensure their survival for future generations. Understanding and preserving the African elephant is vital for maintaining the biodiversity and health of their ecosystems.

**Text 2: The North American Beaver**

The North American beaver is a fascinating and industrious mammal known for its remarkable ability to transform its environment. Found throughout North America, these large rodents are primarily located in forests, rivers, and wetlands. Beavers are recognized by their stout bodies, large, flat tails, and prominent orange teeth, which they use to fell trees and build their homes.

Beavers are herbivores, feeding on a variety of vegetation, including tree bark, leaves, twigs, and aquatic plants. They have a unique digestive system that allows them to break down cellulose, a major component of plant cell walls, making them well-adapted to their plant-based diet.

One of the most notable behaviors of beavers is their dam-building. Beavers build dams across streams and rivers using branches, mud, and stones. These dams create ponds that provide protection from predators and a stable habitat for their lodges. Lodges are dome-shaped structures made from sticks and mud, with underwater entrances to keep out intruders. Inside, beavers create dry, insulated living spaces where they store food and raise their young.

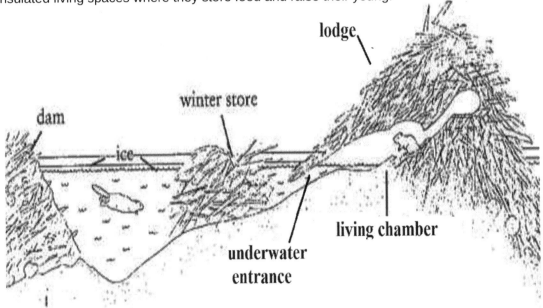

Beavers are known as "ecosystem engineers" because of their significant impact on their surroundings. By building dams, they create wetlands, which serve as important habitats for a variety of species, including fish, birds, and amphibians. Wetlands also help to filter and purify water, control floods, and recharge groundwater supplies.

Socially, beavers live in family groups called colonies, typically consisting of a monogamous pair and their offspring from the past two years. Beavers are highly territorial and use scent marking to defend their territories from other beaver families.

Despite their ecological importance, beavers were once extensively hunted for their fur and castoreum, a substance used in perfumes and medicines. This led to a drastic decline in their population. However, conservation efforts and changes in trapping regulations have helped beaver populations to recover in many areas. Understanding the role of beavers in maintaining healthy ecosystems highlights the importance of preserving these industrious animals.

**21.** Which of the following statements best describes the primary role of the matriarch in an African elephant herd?

A) The matriarch leads the herd, makes decisions, and ensures the safety and well-being of its members.

B) The matriarch helps the herd find food and water and protects them from danger.

C) The matriarch teaches young elephants important survival skills and organizes group activities.

D) The matriarch oversees the herd's daily movements and communicates with other herds.

**22.** Which of the following statements best describes the ecological role of North American beavers as "ecosystem engineers"?

A) Beavers create channels that improve water flow and help transport materials within their habitat.

B) Beavers use their lodges to store food for the winter, ensuring survival during colder months.

C) Beavers construct dams to reduce the flow of rivers, creating ponds that support diverse ecosystems.

D) Beavers build dams that create wetlands, providing habitats for various species and helping to purify water.

**23.** Which of the following statements best explains a similarity between African elephants and North American beavers?

A) Both African elephants and North American beavers build structures to protect themselves from predators.

B) Both African elephants and North American beavers are herbivores and play crucial roles in their ecosystems.

C) Both African elephants and North American beavers live in solitary conditions and only come together for breeding.

D) Both African elephants and North American beavers migrate long distances to find food and water.

**24.** What do African elephants primarily use their trunks for?

A) Digging

B) Building

C) Breathing

D) Drinking

**25.** Which of the following best describes a key difference between the habitats of African elephants and North American beavers?

- (A) African elephants live in wetlands, while North American beavers live in deserts.
- (B) African elephants thrive in savannas, forests, and deserts, while North American beavers are found in forests, rivers, and wetlands.
- (C) African elephants build dams in forests, while North American beavers build lodges in savannas.
- (D) African elephants migrate to wetlands during the winter, while North American beavers stay in forests.

**26.** How do the social structures of African elephants and North American beavers differ in terms of family organization?

- (A) African elephants live in solitary conditions, while North American beavers form large herds.
- (B) African elephants form herds led by a matriarch, while North American beavers live in family groups called colonies.
- (C) African elephants live in small nests, while North American beavers build large lodges for multiple families.
- (D) African elephants migrate alone, while North American beavers travel in pairs.

**27.** What might be the long-term ecological impact if the populations of both African elephants and North American beavers were to decline significantly?

- (A) There would be no noticeable impact on their ecosystems.
- (B) The decline in elephant populations would lead to overgrown savannas, while a decline in beaver populations would result in fewer wetlands, affecting water quality and habitat availability for various species.
- (C) Both African elephants and North American beavers would be easily replaced by other species with no significant changes to the ecosystem.
- (D) The decline in both species would lead to an increase in predator populations in their respective habitats.

**28.** Which of the following best explains how beavers contribute to water purification in their habitats?

- (A) Beavers build dams that slow down water flow, allowing sediments and pollutants to settle, which purifies the water.
- (B) Beavers dig channels that redirect water away from polluted areas.
- (C) Beavers remove debris from rivers and streams, making the water cleaner.
- (D) Beavers drink large amounts of water, reducing pollution levels.

**29.** Explain how both African elephants and North American beavers impact their ecosystems. Provide one specific example from each animal to support your explanation.

_____

_____

_____

_____

_____

_____

_____

_____

_____

_____

_____

**30.** Write a detailed essay analyzing the impact of African elephants and North American beavers on their ecosystems. Evaluate how their roles as "ecosystem engineers" contribute to biodiversity and the health of their environments. Consider the consequences if these species were to decline significantly or become extinct. Use specific examples from the texts to support your analysis and include relevant vocabulary.

_____

_____

_____

**Read the literary text and answer items 31 - 40.**

### A Rainy Day Adventure

The rain poured down in heavy sheets, drumming against the windows of the small house where Sam and Lily lived. The siblings sat by the living room window, watching the water splash into puddles and run down the street in little rivers. It was a Saturday, and their plans to play outside had been washed away by the storm.

"Looks like we're stuck inside all day," Sam sighed, pressing his nose against the glass. "Maybe we can find something fun to do indoors," Lily suggested, her eyes bright with ideas.

Their mom walked in, carrying a basket of laundry. "Why don't you two use your imagination? Rainy days can be just as adventurous as sunny ones," she said, smiling.

Sam and Lily exchanged a look. "What kind of adventure can we have inside?" Sam asked, doubtfully.

"I have an idea!" Lily exclaimed. "Let's build a fort!"

The siblings hurried to gather blankets, pillows, and chairs from around the house. Soon, they had constructed a grand fort in the middle of the living room. The blanket roof sagged in the middle, but to Sam and Lily, it was perfect. They crawled inside, bringing along their favourite books, a flashlight, and a plate of cookies their mom had baked earlier.

"This is awesome," Sam said, biting into a cookie. "It's like we're explorers on a rainy expedition."

"Exactly!" Lily agreed, flipping open a book. "And look, we have plenty of stories to keep us entertained."

As they read, the sound of the rain outside became a comforting background noise, like a steady drumbeat. The fort felt warm and safe, a cozy refuge from the storm.

Lily's eyes sparkled. "Yes! I'll be Captain Lily, the brave explorer. And you can be Sam, the clever inventor."
Sam grinned. "Okay. Captain Lily and Sam the Inventor, on a mission to find the lost treasure of Rainy Island."

They took turns adding to the story, their imaginations painting vivid pictures of dense jungles, hidden caves, and treacherous cliffs. In their tale, the rain became a magical force, guiding them to the treasure. Each new twist and turn in their adventure brought them closer together, filling the fort with laughter and excitement.

Suddenly, their mom's voice interrupted their adventure. "Time for lunch, explorers!"

Reluctantly, Sam and Lily crawled out of the fort, but they carried the spirit of their adventure with them to the kitchen. Over sandwiches and soup, they recounted the details of their story to their mom, who listened with a smile.

"That sounds like an incredible journey," she said. "See? Rainy days aren't so bad after all."

After a while, Sam put down his book and said, "Let's make up our own story. We can be the characters."

After lunch, the rain began to ease up, but Sam and Lily decided to stay indoors. They returned to their fort and continued their adventure, the sound of the raindrops now a gentle patter against the windows.

As the day drew to a close, Sam looked at his sister and said, "I think rainy days might be my new favourite."

Lily nodded, her face glowing with happiness. "Me too. Rainy days are for adventures, and we can have them anytime, right here."

And so, Sam and Lily discovered that even the stormiest days could be filled with magic and adventure, as long as they had each other and a little bit of imagination.

**31.** Who suggests using their imagination to find something fun to do indoors?

- (A) Sam
- (B) Lily
- (C) Their mom
- (D) Their dad

**32.** In the context of the story, what does the word "refuge" most likely mean?

- (A) A place of danger
- (B) A place of safety
- (C) A place of boredom
- (D) A place of entertainment

**33.** How does the use of the word "expedition" enhance the description of Sam and Lily's activity?

- (A) It suggests they are bored and looking for something to do.
- (B) It emphasizes their need to stay indoors due to the rain.
- (C) It adds a sense of adventure and excitement to their fort-building.
- (D) It indicates that they are reading books about explorers.

**34.** Which event in the story shows Sam and Lily's initial disappointment with the rainy day?

- (A) They gather materials to build a fort.
- (B) They eat cookies their mom baked earlier.
- (C) They decide to read books in the living room.
- (D) They press their noses against the window and sigh.

**35.** Why do Sam and Lily decide to stay indoors even after the rain begins to ease up?

- (A) They are too tired to go outside.
- (B) They are afraid it will start raining again.
- (C) Their mom tells them to stay inside.
- (D) They want to finish their adventure story.

**36.** How does the theme of imagination help Sam and Lily turn a rainy day into an adventure?

- (A) A place of dangerIt encourages them to read more books about explorers.
- (B) It helps them ignore the rain and focus on outdoor activities.
- (C) It allows them to create a fun and engaging story indoors.
- (D) It makes them appreciate the rain for watering the plants.

**37.** What does the siblings' ability to turn a rainy day into a fun adventure suggest about the importance of imagination in dealing with unexpected situations?

- (A) Imagination allows people to find joy and creativity in any circumstance.
- (B) Imagination is only useful for creating stories and games.
- (C) Imagination can help people ignore problems entirely.
- (D) Imagination makes it easier to avoid responsibilities during difficult times.

**38.** How does the dialogue between Sam and Lily contribute to the development of the theme of creativity?

- (A) It shows that they are bored and have nothing to do.
- (B) It highlights their ability to work together and come up with imaginative ideas.
- (C) It indicates that they prefer reading books over playing outside.
- (D) It reveals their disappointment with the rain.

**27.** Evaluate the effectiveness of the fort-building activity in changing Sam and Lily's perspective on the rainy day. How does this activity demonstrate the importance of imagination and adaptability in overcoming challenges? Use examples from the text to support your analysis.

(A) The fort-building was not very effective because they were still disappointed by the rain.

(B) The fort-building was effective because it allowed them to have fun and create an adventure, showing how imagination and adaptability can turn a negative situation into a positive one.

(C) The fort-building was somewhat effective, but they still wished they could play outside.

(D) The fort-building was effective only because it provided them with a temporary distraction from

**40.** In the story "A Rainy Day Adventure," Sam and Lily demonstrate the themes of creativity and adaptability in the face of an unexpected rainy day. Discuss how these themes are developed throughout the story, using specific examples from the text to support your analysis. How can the lessons learned from Sam and Lily's experience be applied to real-life situations where plans are disrupted?

In your response, be sure to:
1. Identify and explain the themes of creativity and adaptability as presented in the story.
2. Provide at least three specific examples from the text that illustrate these themes.
3. Discuss how these themes can be applied to real-life situations, giving at least one
4. detailed example.
5. Conclude by summarizing the importance of creativity and adaptability in overcoming
6. challenges.

Read the poem and answer items 41 - 51.

### The Dance of Butterflies

In a garden bright with morning's gleam,
Soft wings flutter, like a dream.
Butterflies dance on petals light,
A waltz of colours, pure delight.

Their wings, a tapestry so fine,
With hues that shimmer, intertwine.
From flower to flower, they softly glide,
Nature's painters on the breeze they ride.

Metamorphosis, their secret spell,
From caterpillar's silent shell.
They shed the old, embrace the new,
A life reborn in morning dew.

Their fragile beauty speaks to me,
Of change, of hope, of being free.
In silence, they do teach and guide,
To trust the journey, time, and tide.

Oh, butterflies, with grace so rare,
You float like whispers in the air.
A lesson in each fleeting flight,
In every dawn, in every night.

**41.** Which of the following best describes the theme of the poem "The Dance of Butterflies"?

(A) The importance of gardens in nature

(B) The process of butterfly metamorphosis

(C) The beauty and symbolism of butterflies

(D) The different colors of butterfly wings

**42.** According to the poem "The Dance of Butterflies," what do butterflies symbolize?

A) Strength and power

B) Change and hope

C) Silence and secrecy

D) Joy and laughter

**43.** How does the poet use imagery to convey the beauty of butterflies in "The Dance of Butterflies"?

A) By comparing their flight to a "whisper in the air"

B) By describing their wings as "fragile" and "delicate"

C) By explaining the process of metamorphosis in detail

D) By stating that butterflies teach and guide us

**44.** In the poem "The Dance of Butterflies," what does the word "metamorphosis" mean?

A) A change in the weather

B) A process of transformation

C) A type of butterfly dance

D) A kind of flower

**45.** What is the effect of using the word "tapestry" in the poem "The Dance of Butterflies"?

A) It highlights the complexity and beauty of butterfly wings.

B) It describes the physical strength of butterflies.

C) It suggests that butterflies are like pieces of fabric.

D) It emphasizes the size and shape of the butterflies.

**46.** How does the poet's use of the word "whisper" in the line "You float like whispers in the air" affect the tone of the poem?

- A  It creates a sense of mystery.
- B  It conveys a feeling of gentleness and delicacy.
- C  It adds a sense of urgency.
- D  It emphasizes the loudness of the butterflies.

**47.** How does the poet's description of butterflies as "Nature's painters" contribute to the theme of the poem?

- A  It emphasizes the artistic and creative qualities of nature.
- B  It highlights the beautiful aspects of butterflies.
- C  It suggests that butterflies are similar to human artists.
- D  It indicates that butterflies create actual paintings.

**48.** In what way does the poet use the butterfly's life cycle to symbolize personal growth in the poem?

- A  By showing how butterflies help flowers grow.
- B  By focusing on the butterfly's diet.
- C  By describing the butterfly's colors.
- D  By illustrating the stages from caterpillar to butterfly as stages of human development.

**49.** Consider the poem's use of metamorphosis as a central metaphor. How might this metaphor be applied to real-life experiences of change and growth? Support your answer with examples from both the poem and your own experiences or observations.

- A  It shows how scientific processes are important.
- B  It suggests that all changes are difficult and painful.
- C  It illustrates that change, though challenging, can lead to beautiful and positive outcomes.
- D  It implies that only physical changes are significant.

**50.** Explain how the poet uses imagery and symbolism in "The Dance of Butterflies" to convey themes of change and beauty. Provide specific examples from the poem to support your explanation.

_____

_____

_____

_____

_____

_____

_____

_____

_____

**51.** Analyze how the poet's choice of words and phrases in "The Dance of Butterflies" helps to convey the themes of transformation and hope. Use specific examples from the poem to support your analysis.

_____

_____

_____

_____

_____

_____

_____

# Answers Test Practice 4

1. C. A visit to the Melody Library.
2. B. By encouraging students to share and perform music from their cultural backgrounds.
3. A. Music can help people remember their heritage and learn about others.
4. B. A handwritten or typed document.
5. D. It suggests that music is a container that holds and transports knowledge across time.
6. C. By highlighting the project where students share music from their cultures and learn about each other's histories.
7. A. Music is an essential part of the town's identity and daily life.
8. B. "The notes flowed like a gentle stream, each one carrying a piece of her thoughts, dreams, and curiosities."
9. ● 2 marks: Response provides a detailed analysis of how Maya's interactions with the community illustrate the theme of music as a unifying force, with specific details from the story. It explains how these interactions help Maya and her classmates understand the broader significance of music.
● 1 mark: Response provides a basic analysis with some mention of Maya's interactions and the theme of music as a unifying force, supported by at least
one detail from the story. It touches on how these interactions help with
understanding music's significance.
● 0 marks: Response does not provide an analysis or lacks specific details from
the story.
10. 2 marks: Response thoroughly describes Maya's transformation in understanding and appreciating music, supported by specific examples from her interactions and actions in the story. It explains how her experiences in Harmony Springs shape her perception of music's importance in society.
1 mark: Response provides a basic description of Maya's transformation with some examples from the story. It mentions how her experiences shape her perception of music's importance.
0 marks: The response does not describe Maya's transformation or lacks specific examples from the story.
11. B. Radio
12. D. Shawn Fanning
13. A. Magnetic Tape
14. B Compact Discs
15. C. Made it easier to share and download music.
16. C. Provided instant access to millions of songs.
17. A. DAWs have allowed musicians to create, edit and produce music
18. C. CDs offered better sound quality and durability, while MP3s revolutionized music distribution by making it easy to share and download music over the Internet.
19. Students should describe how magnetic tape allowed for higher-quality recordings.
Mention that multitrack recording enabled artists to record different parts of a song separately and mix them together.
Provide an example from the text, such as Les Paul's contribution to multitrack recording and his quote, "You can make things sound a lot more like what you hear in your head."
Students should discuss the impact on the complexity and polish of music productions.
20. Students should describe how streaming services like Spotify, Apple Music, and YouTube provide instant access to millions of songs.
Mention Daniel Ek's quote, "We want to create a service that takes the complexity out of the music experience."
Compare this to earlier advancements, such as the introduction of the radio, which made music accessible in homes, and MP3s, which allowed easy sharing and downloading of music.
Evaluate the overall impact, including the accessibility and convenience of streaming services versus the physical media like records and CDs.
Discuss how streaming services have made music more globally accessible without the need for physical products.
21. A. The matriarch leads the herd, makes decisions, and ensures the safety and well-being of its members.
22. D. Beavers build dams that create wetlands, providing habitats for various species and helping to purify water.
23. B. Both African elephants and North American beavers are herbivores and play crucial roles in their ecosystems.
24. C. Breathing
25. B. African elephants thrive in savannas, forests, and deserts, while North American beavers are found in forests, rivers, and wetlands.
26. B. African elephants form herds led by a matriarch, while North American beavers live in family groups called colonies.
27. B. The decline in elephant populations would lead to overgrown savannas, while a decline in beaver populations would result in fewer wetlands, affecting water quality and habitat availability for various species.
28. A. Beavers build dams that slow down water flow, allowing sediments and pollutants to settle, which purifies the water.
29. ● African elephants impact their ecosystems by helping to shape the landscape. They do this by uprooting trees and shrubs, which helps to maintain the savanna ecosystem and allows grasses to grow. This benefits other species that rely on open grasslands.
● North American beavers impact their ecosystems by building dams, which create wetlands. These wetlands provide habitats for various species, help to filter and purify water, and control flooding.
**Marks:**
● 1 mark for correctly explaining the impact of African elephants on their ecosystem with a specific example.
● 1 mark for correctly explaining the impact of North American beavers on their ecosystem with a specific example.
30
**Introduction (1 mark)**
● Define the concept of "ecosystem engineers."
● Introduce African elephants and North American beavers as examples of
ecosystem engineers.
**Body Paragraphs**
**Impact on Ecosystems (2 marks)**
● African Elephants: Analyze how their activities (uprooting trees, maintaining savannas) shape the landscape and promote biodiversity. Provide examples of species that benefit from these changes.
● North American Beavers: Discuss how their dam-building creates wetlands that support diverse species and improve water quality. Include specific examples of benefits to the ecosystem.
**Contribution to Biodiversity (2 marks)**
● Explain the importance of biodiversity in ecosystems.
● African Elephants: Evaluate how their role in maintaining open grasslands contributes to a diverse range of plant and animal species.
● North American Beavers: Assess how the wetlands created by beavers support various life forms and contribute to ecosystem health.

113

Consequences of Decline or Extinction (2 marks)
- African Elephants: Analyze the potential impacts on the savanna ecosystem and other species if elephant populations were to decline or become extinct. Consider changes in vegetation and habitat loss for other species.
- North American Beavers: Evaluate the consequences for wetland ecosystems and species reliant on these habitats if beaver populations were to decline or become extinct. Consider the effects on water quality and flood control.

Conclusion (1 mark)
- Summarize the key points made in the essay.
- Emphasize the importance of conservation efforts to protect both species and their ecosystems.

Use of Relevant Vocabulary (1 mark)
- Ensure the use of specific vocabulary from the texts, such as "herbivores," "ecosystem engineers," "wetlands," "savanna," "biodiversity," "conservation," and "habitats."

31.C. Their mom
32.B. A place of safety
33.C. It adds a sense of adventure and excitement to their fort-building.
34.D. They press their noses against the window and sigh.
35.D. They want to finish their adventure story.
36.C. It allows them to create a fun and engaging story indoors.
37.A. Imagination allows people to find joy and creativity in any circumstance.
38.B. It highlights their ability to work together and come up with imaginative ideas.
39.B. The fort-building was effective because it allowed them to have fun and create an adventure, showing how imagination and adaptability can turn a negative situation into a positive one.
40.In "A Rainy Day Adventure," Sam and Lily transform a disappointing rainy day into a fun and imaginative experience, illustrating the themes of creativity and adaptability. They creatively use household items to build a fort and invent an adventurous story about finding lost treasure, turning their indoor activity into an exciting adventure. Their adaptability is shown when they adjust their plans due to the rain, embracing the challenge and finding joy indoors. This story demonstrates how imagination and flexibility can help overcome unexpected situations, turning potential disappointments into memorable experiences. In real life, these themes encourage us to find innovative solutions and maintain a positive attitude when plans go awry.
41.C. The beauty and symbolism of butterflies
42.B. Change and hope
43.A. By comparing their flight to a "whisper in the air"
44.B. A process of transformation
45.A. It highlights the complexity and beauty of butterfly wings.
46.B. It conveys a feeling of gentleness and delicacy.
47.A. It emphasizes the artistic and creative qualities of nature.
48.D. By illustrating the stages from caterpillar to butterfly as stages of human development.
49.C. It illustrates that change, though challenging, can lead to beautiful and positive outcomes.
50.**1 Mark:** Clear explanation of how the poet uses imagery to convey the theme of beauty, with specific examples (e.g., "Soft wings flutter, like a dream" and "A waltz of colours, pure delight").
**1 Mark:** Clear explanation of how the poet uses symbolism to convey the theme of change, with specific examples (e.g., "Metamorphosis, their secret spell" and "They shed the old, embrace the new").
51.1 Mark: Explanation of how the poet's choice of words and phrases conveys the theme of transformation. Example: The use of words like "metamorphosis" and
phrases such as "shed the old, embrace the new" highlights the process of change and renewal.
1 Mark: Explanation of how the poet's choice of words and phrases conveys the theme of hope. Example: Phrases like "trust the journey" and "a life reborn in morning dew" suggest optimism and the potential for new beginnings.

**Read the information text and answer items 1 - 10.**

## Restoration of Old Buildings

Restoring old buildings is a fascinating and important process. It involves repairing and preserving structures that have historical, cultural, or architectural significance. Imagine an old library that your grandparents might have used or a church that's stood in your town for hundreds of years. These buildings are pieces of our history and restoring them helps keep our past alive for future generations.

Restoration is different from renovation. Renovation means updating a building, often changing its style or purpose. Restoration, on the other hand, focuses on returning a building to its original condition. This can include fixing the roof, repairing walls, and even finding old furniture that matches the building's time period.

One important reason to restore old buildings is to preserve history. Each building tells a story about the time when it was built. For example, the Liberty Bell in Philadelphia is housed in a restored building. This site helps us learn about American history and the struggle for independence.

Restoring buildings also helps protect the environment. Instead of demolishing old structures and building new ones, which uses a lot of resources and creates waste, restoration uses fewer materials and can even improve a building's energy efficiency. This is a form of recycling that reduces the need for new construction materials and helps decrease our carbon footprint.

Another reason for restoring old buildings is to boost local economies. Restored buildings often become tourist attractions, bringing visitors to a town or city. This can create jobs and support local businesses. For instance, the restoration of the Fox Theatre in Atlanta has made it a popular destination, attracting thousands of visitors each year.

The process of restoration involves several steps. First, experts study the building to understand its history and condition. They look at old photos, drawings, and documents to learn how it originally looked. Then, they make a plan to fix any damage while preserving as much of the original structure as possible. Skilled workers, like carpenters, masons, and painters, carefully do the repairs using traditional materials and techniques.

Restoring old buildings is not always easy. It can be expensive and time-consuming. However, many people believe it is worth the effort to save these important parts of our heritage. Organizations like the National Trust for Historic Preservation work hard to protect and restore historic places across the United States.

In conclusion, restoring old buildings is a way to honor our history, protect the environment, and support local economies. By learning about and preserving these structures, we keep our connection to the past strong and ensure that future generations can enjoy and learn from them.

1. **Which of the following is a primary reason for restoring old buildings?**

   (A) To change their style and purpose

   (B) To demolish and rebuild them

   (C) To preserve history and maintain its original condition

   (D) To use modern construction materials

115

**2.** What organization is mentioned as working to protect and restore historic places in the United States?

( A )  National Park Service

( B )  National Trust for Historic Preservation

( C )  Historical Society of America

( D )  American Heritage Foundation

**3.** How does restoring old buildings help protect the environment?

( A )  It reduces the need for new construction materials and decreases waste.

( B )  It uses modern construction materials that are environmentally friendly.

( C )  It involves demolishing old structures to make space for parks.

( D )  It promotes the use of old furniture to match the building's time period.

**4.** Why is it beneficial for local economies to restore old buildings?

( A )  It allows for the construction of new businesses in place of the old buildings.

( B )  It reduces the cost of materials needed for construction.

( C )  It attracts tourists, creating jobs and supporting local businesses.

( D )  It simplifies the planning and building process for new projects.

**5.** What does the term "restoration" mean when referring to old buildings?

( A )  Adding new rooms to a building

( B )  Painting the exterior of a building

( C )  Installing modern technology in a building

( D )  Returning a building to its original condition

6. How does understanding the difference between "restoration" and "renovation" help in planning the preservation of historic buildings?

   A ) It helps determine the budget needed for the project.

   B ) It guides the choice of materials and techniques used.

   C ) It ensures that modern features are added to the building.

   D ) It identifies the historical significance of the building.

7. Why might experts study old photos, drawings, and documents before restoring a building?

   A ) To decide which modern features to add

   B ) To determine how to completely change the building

   C ) To understand the building's original appearance and condition

   D ) To find ways to save money on materials

8. Explain how restoring old buildings can have long-term benefits for a community. Provide at least two examples from the text to support your explanation.

_____

_____

_____

_____

_____

_____

_____

_____

_____

_____

_____

**9.** Describe the process of restoring an old building. Why is it important to use traditional materials and techniques during this process? Use details from the text to support your response.

_____

_____

_____

_____

_____

_____

_____

_____

**10.** How does restoring old buildings contribute to both preserving history and protecting the environment? Use specific examples from the text to explain your answer.

_____

_____

_____

_____

_____

_____

_____

_____

**Charlie Chaplin, Silent Star**

In black and white, he graced the screen,
A funny man, so smart and keen.
With bowler hat and cane in hand,
He made the world laugh, oh so grand.

No words he spoke, but faces told,
A million tales, both shy and bold.
His little tramp, with shoes too big,
Danced and twirled, a joyful jig.

Through laughter, tears, and every scene,
He taught us all what kindness means.
Charlie Chaplin, a timeless name,
In silent films, he found his fame.

**11.** **Which character is Charlie Chaplin most famous for portraying in his silent films?**

A    A king

B    A little tramp

C    A magician

D    A cowboy

**12.** **What did Charlie Chaplin use to make the world laugh without speaking?**

A    His dancing and twirling

B    His colorful costumes

C    His silent voice

D    His magic trick

**13.** What message does the poem suggest Charlie Chaplin conveyed through his performances?

A  The importance of wealth

B  The power of kindness

C  The thrill of adventure

D  The joy of winning

**14.** Which detail from the poem best shows that Charlie Chaplin was a successful entertainer?

A  "In black and white, he graced the screen"

B  "With bowler hat and cane in hand"

C  "He made the world laugh, oh so grand"

D  "His little tramp, with shoes too big"

**15.** What does the word "timeless" in the last line of the poem most likely mean?

A  Old-fashioned

B  Temporary

C  Always relevant

D  Forgotten

**16.** How does the poet's use of the word "keen" to describe Charlie Chaplin affect the reader's understanding of his character?

A  t shows that Charlie Chaplin was very serious and strict.

B  It suggests that Charlie Chaplin was intelligent and perceptive.

C  It implies that Charlie Chaplin was always in a hurry.

D  It indicates that Charlie Chaplin was often confused.

120

**17.** Which line from the poem best illustrates Charlie Chaplin's ability to tell stories without speaking?

- (A) "With bowler hat and cane in hand"
- (B) He made the world laugh, oh so grand"
- (C) "No words he spoke, but faces told"
- (D) "Through laughter, tears, and every scene"

**18.** What might the poem suggest about the importance of non-verbal communication in entertainment?

- (A) It is less effective than verbal communication.
- (B) It can transcend language barriers and connect with a wider audience.
- (C) It is only suitable for silent films.
- (D) It is often misunderstood by audiences.

**19.** How does the poet use imagery to convey Charlie Chaplin's impact on the audience? Provide specific examples from the poem to support your answer.

_____

_____

_____

_____

_____

_____

_____

_____

_____

_____

**20.** Explain how the poem describes Charlie Chaplin's ability to communicate and entertain without using words. Use specific details from the poem to support your answer.

**Read the two texts and answer items 21 - 30.**

### All About Dogs

Dogs are one of the most popular pets in the world, and in my opinion, they are the best pets anyone could ever have. Their loyalty, intelligence, and ability to form close bonds with humans make them truly special. Dogs belong to the Canidae family, which also includes wolves, foxes, and coyotes. With over 340 different dog breeds, each has its own unique and charming characteristics.

Dogs are often referred to as "man's best friend," and I wholeheartedly agree with this sentiment. Their companionship and assistance to humans are unparalleled. Archaeological evidence shows that dogs were domesticated from wolves over 15,000 years ago. This long history of companionship has made dogs an integral and beloved part of many households.

One of the most impressive roles dogs play is as service animals. Service dogs are specially trained to help people with disabilities. For example, guide dogs assist visually impaired individuals, while hearing dogs alert their owners to important sounds. Therapy dogs provide comfort to people in hospitals, nursing homes, and schools, showing just how caring and helpful dogs can be.

Dogs have an extraordinary sense of smell, which makes them invaluable in various fields. They are used by police and military forces to detect drugs, explosives, and even missing persons. Their sense of smell is so powerful that they can detect some diseases, such as cancer, by sniffing human breath or skin. This incredible ability highlights just how amazing dogs truly are.

In my opinion, dogs need proper care to stay healthy and happy, just as they deserve. They require a balanced diet, regular exercise, and veterinary check-ups. Exercise is crucial because it helps prevent obesity and keeps their muscles strong. Additionally, dogs need mental stimulation, such as training and playtime, to keep their minds active and content.

In conclusion, dogs are remarkable animals that contribute significantly to human society. In my view, their loyalty, helpfulness, and companionship make them the best pets anyone could ever have. By understanding and caring for dogs, we can ensure they remain our loyal friends for many years to come. Dogs truly make our lives better, and I believe they deserve all the love and care we can give them.

### All About Cats

Cats are one of the most beloved pets in the world, and in my opinion, they are the best pets anyone could have. Their independence, affectionate nature, and unique personalities make them wonderful companions. Cats belong to the Felidae family, which includes lions, tigers, and leopards. There are over 70 different cat breeds, each with its own distinct traits.

Cats have been domesticated for thousands of years. Archaeological evidence suggests that cats were first domesticated in ancient Egypt around 4,000 years ago. They were highly valued for their ability to control pests like mice and rats. This long history of living alongside humans has made cats cherished members of many households.

One of the reasons cats are such fantastic pets is their independence. Unlike some other pets, cats can be left alone for longer periods, making them ideal for people with busy schedules. They are also very clean animals, grooming themselves regularly to keep their fur neat and tidy.

Cats are known for their playful and curious nature. They love to explore their surroundings and play with toys, which keeps them active and healthy. Their agility and grace are truly remarkable, and watching a cat jump and climb can be mesmerizing. In my opinion, their playful antics bring joy and entertainment to any home.

Cats also have a calming presence. Studies have shown that the sound of a cat's purr can reduce stress and anxiety in humans. Their gentle purring is not only soothing but also has a healing effect. This makes them excellent companions for people who need comfort and relaxation.

In conclusion, cats are amazing animals that make the best pets. Their independence, playful nature, and calming presence make them ideal companions. By understanding and caring for cats, we can ensure they remain our loving friends for many years to come. In my view, cats bring endless joy and comfort to our lives, and they truly deserve to be cherished.

21. **Which of the following statements best explains why dogs are considered valuable in various fields, according to the informational text?**

A   Dogs are known for their ability to form close bonds with humans.

B   Dogs have been domesticated for thousands of years.

C   Dogs have an excellent sense of smell, which makes them valuable in detecting drugs, explosives, and even diseases.

D   Dogs need proper care to stay healthy and happy.

22. **Which of the following statements best explains why cats are considered excellent pets, according to the informational text?**

A   Cats belong to the Felidae family, which includes lions, tigers, and leopards.

B   Cats were first domesticated in ancient Egypt around 4,000 years ago.

C   Cats need regular grooming to keep their fur neat and tidy.

D   Cats are independent, and playful, and have a calming presence that reduces stress and anxiety.

23. **Consider the roles that both dogs and cats play in human society as described in the texts. How do the unique characteristics of dogs and cats contribute differently to their value as pets?**

A   Dogs' sense of smell and training abilities make them useful in law enforcement and as service animals, while cats' independence and grooming habits make them easy to care for and calming companions.

B   Dogs' long history of domestication makes them loyal companions, while cats' playful nature makes them entertaining pets.

C   Dogs require regular exercise and veterinary check-ups, while cats need mental stimulation through playtime and training.

D   Dogs and cats both need balanced diets and regular exercise, which makes them healthy and active pets.

**24.** What is one reason the text gives for why dogs are useful in law enforcement?

- (A) Dogs can be left alone for long periods of time.
- (B) Dogs have an excellent sense of smell.
- (C) Dogs can groom themselves regularly.
- (D) Dogs provide comfort to people in hospitals.

**25.** Which statement best describes the main idea of the text about cats?

- (A) Cats are members of the Felidae family.
- (B) Cats have been domesticated for thousands of years.
- (C) Cats are considered excellent pets due to their independence, cleanliness, and calming presence.
- (D) Cats need regular grooming to keep their fur neat and tidy.

**26.** How does the text explain the calming effect of cats on humans?

- (A) Cats' playful antics bring joy and entertainment to any home.
- (B) Cats' independence makes them ideal for busy people.
- (C) The sound of a cat's purr can reduce stress and anxiety in humans.
- (D) Cats have been domesticated for thousands of years.

**27.** Explain how the unique characteristics of dogs and cats contribute to their roles as pets, according to the texts. Use specific details from the texts to support your answer.

_____

_____

_____

_____

_____

_____

_____

_____

_____

_____

_____

**28.** Both texts argue that dogs and cats make excellent pets, but for different reasons. Evaluate the arguments presented in each text and determine which pet you believe would be the best choice for a busy family. Support your answer with evidence from the texts.

_____

_____

_____

_____

_____

_____

_____

_____

_____

_____

_____

_____

**29.** Using evidence from the informational texts about dogs and cats, explain how the unique characteristics of each animal contribute to their roles as pets and their value to humans. Be sure to include specific examples from the texts to support your response.

_____

_____

_____

_____

_____

_____

_____

_____

_____

**30.** Based on the informational texts about dogs and cats, write an essay discussing which animal you believe makes the best pet. In your essay, consider the unique characteristics and roles of each animal as presented in the texts. Use specific evidence and examples to support your argument. Your essay should be well-organized, with a clear introduction, body paragraphs, and a conclusion.

_____

_____

_____

_____

_____

**Read the information text and answer items 41 - 51.**

### Dancing Through the Storm

It was a gray Tuesday afternoon, and the clouds hung low in the sky, threatening rain. The usually lively hallways of Pinewood Middle School felt subdued as if the building itself was holding its breath. In Classroom 6B, however, there was a buzz of excitement.

"Alright, class," Mrs. Thompson called, clapping her hands for attention. "Today, we have a special guest. Please welcome Miss Luna, a professional dancer who will be teaching us about the art of dance."

The students' eyes widened with curiosity and anticipation. Miss Luna, a tall woman with graceful movements, stepped forward. Her warm smile instantly put everyone at ease.

"Hello, everyone," she began. "Dancing is more than just movement. It's a way to express feelings and tell stories. Today, I'm going to show you how to dance through different emotions, even when the world around you feels stormy."

The rain began to patter against the windows as Miss Luna led the class to the gymnasium. The large, open space seemed to amplify the sound of the raindrops, creating a rhythm of its own.

"Let's start with something simple," Miss Luna said. "Imagine you are leaves being blown by the wind. Let your bodies move freely, without thinking too much."

At first, the students felt a bit awkward. They shuffled their feet and glanced at each other uncertainly. But as they watched Miss Luna twirl and sway with the imaginary wind, they began to loosen up. Even quiet Liam, who usually preferred reading to running around, found himself caught up in the moment.

"Good, now think about how you feel on a sunny day," Miss Luna encouraged. "Let that joy and energy flow through your movements."

As they danced, the students' movements became more expressive. Aiden's jumps were full of enthusiasm, reflecting his vibrant personality. Ethan's steps were measured and thoughtful, showing his growing confidence.

"Remember, dance can also tell a story," Miss Luna said, her voice carrying over the steady drumming of the rain. "Let's create a story together. Imagine we're on an adventure, but suddenly, a storm hits. How do you move through the storm?"

The room filled with dramatic movements as the students imagined battling the elements. Dawud, who often struggled to stay focused, moved with intense concentration, his face set in determination. Hlomani, usually reserved, let out a burst of creativity, his steps mirroring the chaos of the storm.

"Feel the power of the storm, but don't let it overwhelm you," Miss Luna guided. "Find your way through it."

As the imaginary storm raged, the students danced with increasing confidence and unity. The sound of their feet echoed in the gym, mingling with the real storm outside. Their movements, initially hesitant, grew bold and assured. They were not just moving; they were communicating, sharing a story of resilience and strength.

Finally, Miss Luna signaled for them to slow down. "Now, let the storm pass," she said softly. "Feel the calm returning. How does your body react?"

Breathing heavily, the students gradually transitioned to gentler movements. The storm, both inside and outside, began to subside. The rain was now a gentle patter, a soothing backdrop to their quiet dance.

"Wonderful," Miss Luna praised, clapping her hands. "You all did an amazing job. Remember, no matter what storms you face, you can always dance through them."

As the class ended, the students felt a new sense of accomplishment. They had danced through the storm, both real and imagined, and discovered a powerful way to express themselves.

In the quiet that followed, Ethan raised his hand. "Miss Luna," he asked, "can we do this again sometime?"

Miss Luna smiled warmly. "Absolutely," she replied. "Dance is always here for you, no matter what."

And with that, the students returned to their classroom, their hearts lighter and their spirits uplifted, ready to face any storm that came their way.

**31.** In the story "Dancing Through the Storm," Miss Luna asks the students to imagine they are leaves being blown by the wind. Which of the following words best describes how the students' movements should be?

(A) Agile

(B) Brisk

(C) Graceful

(D) Suple

**32.** In the story "Dancing Through the Storm," Miss Luna teaches the students to use dance to express their emotions. How do the students' movements change from the beginning to the end of the dance session?

(A) They start with dramatic movements and end with hesitant steps.

(B) They begin with awkward shuffling and end with confident, expressive movements.

(C) They start with fast, energetic jumps and end with slow, calm motions.

(D) They begin with fluid movements and end with rigid, controlled steps.

**33.** In the story "Dancing Through the Storm," what is the main lesson Miss Luna wants the students to learn about dance?

(A) Dance is only about precise movements and technique.

(B) Dance is primarily a competitive activity.

(C) Dance should be performed only in perfect weather conditions.

(D) Dance can help express and manage emotions during difficult times.

**34.** In the story "Dancing Through the Storm," how does the interaction between the students and Miss Luna demonstrate the theme of resilience?

(A) By showing the students learning new dance techniques quickly and effortlessly.

(B) By highlighting how the students express their feelings about the storm through dance.

(C) By illustrating the students' progression from uncertainty to confidence as they follow Miss Luna's guidance.

(D) By focusing on the students' enjoyment of dancing on a rainy day.

**35.** In the story "Dancing Through the Storm," what does Miss Luna mean when she says, "Feel the power of the storm, but don't let it overwhelm you"?

A. The students should dance slowly to avoid getting tired.

B. The students should experience strong emotions but remain in control of their movements.

C. The students should imagine they are running away from the storm.

D. The students should avoid thinking about the storm altogether.

**36.** How does the setting of the story, with the real storm outside, enhance the students' experience of learning to dance through an imaginary storm?

A. It makes the students feel more comfortable and relaxed.

B. It distracts the students from their dance practice.

C. It helps the students connect more deeply with the emotions they are expressing through dance.

D. It makes the students want to stop dancing and watch the storm.

**37.** In the story "Dancing Through the Storm," why is it significant that the students' movements change from hesitant to confident by the end of the session?

A. It shows they have learned the correct dance steps.

B. It indicates their increased understanding of dance as a form of expression.

C. It demonstrates that they prefer dancing to other physical activities.

D. It proves they are no longer afraid of the storm.

**38.** Analyze the role of Miss Luna in transforming the students' perception of dance. How does her approach to teaching help the students develop resilience and emotional expression? Use specific examples from the text to support your answer.

A. Miss Luna's technical expertise in dance helps the students master difficult movements quickly, leading to their confidence.

B. Miss Luna's emphasis on dance as a storytelling and emotional outlet helps the students connect with their feelings and express themselves more openly.

C. Miss Luna's strict rules and focus on perfection force the students to practice diligently and become better dancers.

D. Miss Luna's fun and carefree attitude towards dance makes the students view it as an enjoyable hobby rather than a serious art form.

**39.** In the story "Dancing Through the Storm," how do the students' movements reflect the meaning of the word "resilient"? Use evidence from the text to support your answer.

_____

_____

_____

_____

_____

_____

_____

_____

_____

_____

_____

**40.** In the story "Dancing Through the Storm," Miss Luna helps the students use dance to express their emotions and navigate through challenging situations. Analyze how Miss Luna's guidance impacts the students' understanding of dance and their personal growth. Discuss how her instructions and the students' experiences during the dance session illustrate this impact. Use specific examples from the text to support your analysis.

_____

_____

_____

_____

_____

## The Amazing Octopus

The octopus is a fascinating sea creature known for its intelligence and unique anatomy. Belonging to the class Cephalopoda, octopuses are found in oceans all around the world. Let's dive into what makes the octopus such an extraordinary animal.

First, let's talk about the octopus's body. Unlike fish, octopuses don't have bones. Instead, they have soft, flexible bodies that allow them to squeeze into tiny crevices and hide from predators. Their bodies are covered in special cells called chromatophores, which can change color to blend in with their surroundings. This camouflage helps them avoid being seen by both predators and prey.

An octopus has eight long arms, each covered with suction cups. These suction cups are incredibly strong and help the octopus grasp objects, catch prey, and even walk along the ocean floor. The arms are also very sensitive, allowing the octopus to taste what it touches.

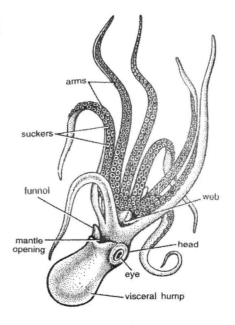

*Octopus.*

Another remarkable feature of the octopus is its beak. Located at the center where all the arms meet, the beak is made of a hard substance called chitin. This beak is very sharp and is used to crack open the shells of crabs, clams, and other shellfish, which are the octopus's main food sources.

Octopuses are known for their intelligence. They have large brains relative to their body size, and they can solve puzzles, navigate mazes, and even use tools. This intelligence helps them find food and avoid dangers in their environment.

In terms of defense, octopuses have a few tricks up their sleeves. If threatened, they can eject a cloud of ink to confuse predators and make a quick escape. Some species can also detach an arm, which will continue to move and distract the predator while the octopus swims away to safety.

In conclusion, the octopus's unique anatomy and intelligence make it one of the most fascinating creatures in the ocean. From its color-changing skin to its powerful arms and sharp beak, every part of the octopus is perfectly adapted to help it survive and thrive in the underwater world.

**41.** **What feature of the octopus helps it blend in with its surroundings?**

A) Its beak

B) Its suction cups

C) Its chromatophores

D) Its ink cloud

**42.** What is the hard substance that makes up an octopus's beak?

- (A) Chitin
- (B) Chromatophores
- (C) Cartilage
- (D) Calcium

**43.** Why are an octopus's suction cups important for its survival?

- (A) They help the octopus change color to blend in with its surroundings.
- (B) They allow the octopus to crack open the shells of its prey.
- (C) They enable the octopus to grasp objects, catch prey, and move along the ocean floor.
- (D) They produce a cloud of ink to confuse predators.

**44.** How does the ability to change color benefit the octopus in its environment?

- (A) It allows the octopus to attract mates.
- (B) It helps the octopus blend in with its surroundings to avoid predators and catch prey.
- (C) It enables the octopus to communicate with other octopuses.
- (D) It allows the octopus to produce a cloud of ink to escape from danger.

**45.** Considering the various features of an octopus, which combination of these features best demonstrates how the octopus avoids predators and finds food in its environment?

- (A) Color-changing skin and suction cups
- (B) Sharp beak and large brain
- (C) Flexible body and ink cloud
- (D) Suction cups and beak

**46.** What role does the octopus's large brain play in its survival?

- (A) It helps the octopus camouflage with its surroundings.
- (B) It enables the octopus to solve puzzles and use tools.
- (C) It allows the octopus to swim faster.
- (D) It helps the octopus produce ink to escape predators.

**47.** How do the octopus's soft, flexible body and ability to squeeze into small crevices benefit its survival in the ocean?

- (A) They help the octopus attract mates.
- (B) They enable the octopus to escape from predators and hide from threats.
- (C) They allow the octopus to swim quickly in open water.
- (D) They help the octopus communicate with other sea creatures.

**48.** Compare the defensive mechanisms of the octopus, such as ejecting ink and detaching an arm, in terms of effectiveness. Which mechanism do you think is more advantageous and why?

_____

_____

_____

_____

_____

_____

_____

_____

_____

_____

**49.** Evaluate how the combination of the octopus's intelligence and physical adaptations enhances its ability to thrive in its environment. Support your evaluation with specific examples from the text.

_____

_____

_____

_____

_____

_____

_____

_____

**50.** Explain how the unique features of an octopus, such as its chromatophores and suction cups, contribute to its survival. Provide specific examples from the text to support your answer.

_____

_____

_____

_____

_____

_____

_____

**51.** Describe the functions of chitin and chromatophores in an octopus. How do these features contribute to the octopus's survival? Provide specific examples from the text to support your answer.

_____

_____

_____

_____

_____

_____

_____

_____

_____

_____

_____

_____

_____

_____

_____

_____

# Answers Test Practice 45

1. C. To preserve history and maintain its original condition
2. B. National Trust for Historic Preservation
3. A. It reduces the need for new construction materials and decreases waste.
4. C. It attracts tourists, creating jobs and supporting local businesses.
5. D. Returning a building to its original condition
6. B. It guides the choice of materials and techniques used.
7. C. To understand the building's original appearance and condition
8. Restoring old buildings can have long-term benefits for a community by preserving its history and boosting the local economy. For example, the restoration of the Fox Theatre in Atlanta has made it a popular tourist destination, attracting thousands of visitors each year and creating jobs. Additionally, preserving historical buildings like the Liberty Bell's housing in Philadelphia helps people learn about and connect with their history, ensuring that important stories and cultural heritage are not lost over time.
9. The process of restoring an old building involves several steps. First, experts study the building to understand its history and condition, looking at old photos, drawings, and documents to learn how it originally looked. Then, they make a plan to fix any damage while preserving as much of the original structure as possible. Skilled workers, such as carpenters, masons, and painters, carefully perform the repairs using traditional materials and techniques.

Using traditional materials and techniques is important because it helps maintain the building's historical integrity and authenticity. It ensures that the restoration is as true to the original construction as possible, preserving the building's historical and cultural significance for future generations. Additionally, using these methods can often be more sustainable and environmentally friendly, as they avoid the use of modern materials that may not be as durable or historically accurate.

10. Restoring old buildings contributes to preserving history by maintaining structures that have historical, cultural, or architectural significance. For example, the Liberty Bell in Philadelphia is housed in a restored building that helps us learn about American history and the struggle for independence. By returning buildings to their original condition, restoration allows us to keep our connection to the past strong.

Restoration also protects the environment by reducing the need for new construction materials and decreasing waste. Instead of demolishing old structures and building new ones, which uses a lot of resources, restoration uses fewer materials. This form of recycling helps decrease our carbon footprint. Restoring buildings can also improve their energy efficiency, further benefiting the environment.

11. B. A little tramp
12. A. His dancing and twirling
13. B. The power of kindness
14. C. "He made the world laugh, oh so grand"
15. C. Always relevant
16. B. It suggests that Charlie Chaplin was intelligent and perceptive.
17. C. "No words he spoke, but faces told"
18. B. It can transcend language barriers and connect with a wider audience.
19. The poet uses vivid imagery to convey Charlie Chaplin's impact on the audience. For instance, the line "He made the world laugh, oh so grand" emphasizes the widespread joy Chaplin brought to people. The imagery of "With bowler hat and cane in hand" creates a visual representation of Chaplin's iconic look, making him easily recognizable. Additionally, "No words he spoke, but faces told" highlights how Chaplin's expressive facial expressions were powerful enough to tell complex stories and evoke emotions. This use of imagery helps the reader understand how Chaplin's silent performances were able to connect deeply with audiences and leave a lasting impression.
20. The poem describes Charlie Chaplin's ability to communicate and entertain without using words through several key details. First, it mentions that he "graced the screen" in "black and white," emphasizing his role in silent films where dialogue was absent. The poem highlights his expressive physical comedy, stating, "With bowler hat and cane in hand, he made the world laugh, oh so grand." This indicates that his actions and gestures were central to his humor. Additionally, the line "No words he spoke, but faces told, a million tales, both shy and bold" shows that his facial expressions were powerful tools in conveying emotions and stories. The poem concludes by noting that through his silent performances, Chaplin "taught us all what kindness means," illustrating that his message was effectively communicated through his non-verbal actions, making his performances timeless and universally understood.
21. C. Dogs have an excellent sense of smell, which makes them valuable in detecting drugs, explosives, and even diseases.
22. D. Cats are independent, playful, and have a calming presence that reduces stress and anxiety.
23. A. Dogs' sense of smell and training abilities make them useful in law enforcement and as service animals, while cats' independence and grooming habits make them easy to care for and calming companions.
24. B. Dogs have an excellent sense of smell.
25. C. Cats are considered excellent pets due to their independence, cleanliness, and calming presence.
26. C. The sound of a cat's purr can reduce stress and anxiety in humans.
27. Dogs' loyalty, intelligence, and exceptional sense of smell make them ideal as service animals and in law enforcement roles. For instance, guide dogs assist visually impaired individuals, and police dogs detect drugs and explosives. Cats, on the other hand, are independent, clean, and have a calming presence. Their ability to groom themselves and their soothing purr, which reduces stress, make them easy to care for and comforting companions.
28. For a busy family, a cat might be the better choice because of its independence and low-maintenance care. The text explains that cats can be left alone for longer periods and groom themselves, making them less demanding on time. Additionally, their calming presence, with the ability to reduce stress through their purring, provides emotional benefits to family members. While dogs offer valuable services and companionship, their need for regular exercise, training, and attention might be challenging for a busy family to manage.
29. Dogs are highly valued for their loyalty, intelligence, and exceptional sense of smell. These traits make them excellent service animals and valuable in law enforcement. For example, guide dogs help individuals who are visually impaired, and police dogs detect drugs and explosives. On the other hand, cats are appreciated for their independence, cleanliness, and calming presence. Their ability to groom themselves and be left alone for longer periods makes them easy to care for, while their purring can reduce stress and anxiety in humans. Both animals offer unique benefits, making them cherished pets in different ways.
30. Introduction
- Briefly introduce the topic of pets, specifically dogs and cats.
- State your opinion on which animal makes the best pet.

Body Paragraph 1: Dogs
- Discuss the unique characteristics of dogs (loyalty, intelligence, sense of smell).
- Provide examples from the text about their roles (service animals, police dogs).
- Explain how these traits make dogs valuable pets.

Body Paragraph 2: Cats
- Discuss the unique characteristics of cats (independence, cleanliness, calming presence).
- Provide examples from the text about their roles (ease of care, stress reduction).
- Explain how these traits make cats valuable pets.

Body Paragraph 3: Comparison and Reasoning
● Compare the characteristics and roles of dogs and cats.
● Explain why one set of characteristics and roles might be more important or beneficial for a pet owner.
● Use specific evidence from the text to support your reasoning.
Conclusion
● Summarize the main points of your essay.
● Restate your opinion on which animal makes the best pet, based on the evidence provided.
Scoring Rubric:
Introduction (1 mark): Clear introduction of the topic and a stated opinion.
Body Paragraph 1 (1 mark): Detailed discussion of dogs' characteristics and roles with specific examples.
36
Body Paragraph 2 (1 mark): Detailed discussion of cats' characteristics and roles with specific examples.
Body Paragraph 3 (2 marks): Effective comparison and reasoning, with evidence from the text.
Conclusion (1 mark): Clear summary and restatement of opinion.
Organization and Clarity (1 mark): Well-organized essay with clear, coherent writing.
31.C. Graceful
32.B.They begin with awkward shuffling and end with confident, expressive movements.
33.D.Dance can help express and manage emotions during difficult times.
34.C.By illustrating the students' progression from uncertainty to confidence as they follow Miss Luna's guidance.
35.B.The students should experience strong emotions but remain in control of their movements.
36.C.It helps the students connect more deeply with the emotions they are expressing through dance.
37.B.It indicates their increased understanding of dance as a form of expression.
38.B.Miss Luna's emphasis on dance as a storytelling and emotional outlet helps the students connect with their feelings and express themselves more openly.
39.1 mark - Correctly explains the meaning of "resilient" and relates it to the students' movements. 1 mark - Provides specific evidence from the text to support the explanations
40.1 mark - Identifies the impact of Miss Luna's guidance on the students. 1 mark - Describes how Miss Luna's instructions help the students understand the expressive nature of dance. 1 mark - Explains the students' experiences and personal growth during the dance session. 1 mark - Uses specific examples from the text to support the analysis of Miss Luna's impact on the students.
41.C.Its chromatophores
42.A.Chtin
43.C.They enable the octopus to grasp objects, catch prey, and move along the ocean floor.
44.B.It helps the octopus blend in with its surroundings to avoid predators and catch prey.
45.A.Color-changing skin and suction cups
46.B. It enables the octopus to solve puzzles and use tools.
47.B.They enable the octopus to escape from predators and hide from threats
48.**1 mark:** Identification of the two defensive mechanisms (ejecting ink and detaching an arm).
**1 mark:** Reasoned argument on which mechanism is more advantageous, with supporting evidence from the text (e.g., ink cloud helps in quick escape by confusing the predator, while detaching an arm distracts the predator).
49.**1 mark:** Explanation of the octopus's intelligence and its role in survival (e.g., solving puzzles, using tools).
**1 mark:** Description of physical adaptations like chromatophores, suction cups, and flexible body.
**2 marks:** Integration of how these features work together to help the octopus find food, avoid predators, and navigate its environment effectively.
50.**1 mark:**Explanation of how chromatophores help the octopus survive (e.g., by changing color to blend in with its surroundings and avoid predators).
**1 mark**: Explanation of how suction cups help the octopus survive (e.g., by allowing it to grasp objects, catch prey, and move along the ocean floor).
51.**1 mark:**Explanation of the function of chitin in an octopus (e.g., chitin makes up the hard beak, which is used to crack open shells of prey)
**1 mark:** Explanation of the function of chromatophores in an octopus (e.g., chromatophores allow the octopus to change color and blend in with its surroundings to avoid predators and catch prey).

Made in the USA
Columbia, SC
15 April 2025

56615730R00080